SERVING THE LORD

Freddie Patrick and Janet Stewart Moon

SERVING THE LORD

*A Festschrift for Freddie Patrick Moon and
Janet Stewart Moon*

EDITORS OF HERITAGE CHRISTIAN
UNIVERSITY PRESS

Copyright © 2022 by Editors of the Heritage Christian University Press

Cataloging-in-Publication Data

Serving the Lord: festschrift for Freddie Patrick Moon and Janet Stewart Moon / by editors of Heritage Christian University Press.

p. cm. (Heritage Legacy Series).

Includes Scripture index.

ISBN 978-1-956811-10-0(hbk,); 978-1-956811-11-7 (ebook)

1. Bible—Criticism, interpretation, etc. 2. Evangelistic work. I. Moon, Freddie Patrick. II Moon, Janet Stewart. III. Title. IV. Series

081—dc20

Library of Congress Control Number: 2021922968

Cover design by Brad McKinnon and Brittany Vander Maas.

For information:

HCU Press
3625 Helton Drive
PO Box HCU
Florence, AL 35630

www.hcu.edu

CONTENTS

WORKS OF
FREDDIE PATRICKMOON

Administrator

Artisan

Craftsman

Stonemason

Master Griller

WORKS OF
JANET STEWART MOON

Photo with Santa

Harvester's Banquet

Heritage Associates

Hospitality Coordinator

Golf Tournament

Founders Day

Heritage Event

Greeting

TRIBUTE

Pat Moon's knowledge of Heritage Christian University began when he worked as an accountant for the late William Britton, who served on the HCU Board of Directors. In 2000, Pat left his role with Muscle Shoals Mack Sales to become HCU's controller. In 2010, he became Vice President of Operations, and in 2019 he was named Senior Vice President for Administration.

Pat's efforts secured impressive funding for HCU from the Gulf Oil Crisis settlement in 2015—weeks of painstaking work documented the economic impact of the spill on the university, opening the door to financial relief. He spearheaded the effort to retire HCU's long-term debt in 2017–18. Pat is also a major force behind HCU's annual Founders Day and the accompanying Founders Day Awards.

Janet began officially working with HCU in 2002 within the Advancement Department. She currently serves as Director of Community Relations. Her roles include directing the annual Harvesters Banquet, coordinating the annual golf tournament, planning meals and social events, and serving as liaison between the Heritage Associates and the university. The Associates rely on Janet to help get major plans into effective action. As a team, Pat and Janet continue to play crucial roles in the annual Heritage Event and various HCU Partnership Dinners.

In addition to administrative duties, Pat is a skilled woodworker. He built the worktables that patrons of the Overton Memorial Library find so useful. He has built speaker stands. Only Travis Harmon could match Pat's sweat equity in the McCreary Cabins. Pat also possesses impressive skills with photography. He has digitally captured numerous events within the Overton Memorial Library.

Travis Harmon, who served as the project manager for McCreary Cabins, said,

> Pat and Janet Moon were the reason that the cabins turned out so amazingly well. There is not a part of the project that they were not involved in. They worked six days a week an entire summer to hang the tongue-and-groove pine on every wall and ceiling. They hung fixtures and wired outlets; they secured donations that allowed the heating and cooling and plumbing to be finished far below the standard cost. I have seen them work tirelessly in the heat, building decks and doing landscaping. There is no doubt that we would have ended up with a more expensive yet inferior product without their sacrificial service. I have seen both of them

working when they were physically injured, sick, and hurting, but they refused to quit until the task was complete because they believe in the mission of HCU.

Pat and Janet are beloved members of the Highland Park Church of Christ. They visit and encourage; they are particularly known for their world-class chocolate pies. The Moons have four children and five grandchildren, who are loved with great heart.

LIST OF CONTRIBUTORS

Bill Bagents is Professor of Ministry, Counseling, and Biblical Studies at Heritage Christian University, Florence, Alabama, USA.

Cory Collins is Pulpit Minister for the Keller Church of Christ, Keller, Texas, USA.

Jamie Cox is Director of Library Services at Heritage Christian University, Florence, Alabama, USA.

Nathan B. Daily is Associate Professor of Religion / Associate Dean / Register at Heritage Christian University, Florence, Alabama, USA.

Ed Gallagher is Professor of Christian Scripture at Heritage Christian University, Florence, Alabama, USA.

Travis Harmon is Vice President of Student Services at Heritage Christian University, Florence, Alabama, USA.

Michael D. Jackson is Vice President of Academic Affairs / Academic Dean at Heritage Christian University, Florence, Alabama, USA.

Brad McKinnon is Associate Professor of History at Heritage Christian University, Florence, Alabama, USA.

Coy D. Roper is retired Professor at Heritage Christian University, Florence, Alabama, USA.

Keith Stanglin is Professor of Theology at Heritage Christian University, Florence, Alabama, USA.

Dianne Tays is Business Office Clerk at Heritage Christian University, Florence, Alabama, USA.

BIBLE ABBREVIATIONS

Old Testament

Gen	Genesis
Exod	Exodus
Lev	Leviticus
Num	Numbers
Deut	Deuteronomy
Josh	Joshua
Judg	Judges
Ruth	Ruth
1–2 Sam	1–2 Samuel
1–2 Kgs	1–2 Kings
1–2 Chr	1–2 Chronicles
Ezra	Ezra
Neh	Nehemiah
Esth	Esther
Job	Job
Ps	Psalms
Prov	Proverbs

Eccl	Ecclesiastes
Song	Song of Solomon
Isa	Isaiah
Jer	Jeremiah
Lam	Lamentations
Ezek	Ezekiel
Dan	Daniel
Hos	Hosea
Joel	Joel
Amos	Amos
Obad	Obadiah
Jonah	Jonah
Mic	Micah
Nah	Nahum
Hab	Habakkuk
Zeph	Zephaniah
Hag	Haggai
Zech	Zechariah
Mal	Malachi

New Testament

Matt	Matthew
Mark	Mark
Luke	Luke
John	John
Acts	Acts
Rom	Romans
1–2 Cor	1–2 Corinthians
Gal	Galatians
Eph	Ephesians
Phil	Philippians

Col	Colossians
1–2 Thess	1–2 Thessalonians
1–2 Tim	1–2 Timothy
Titus	Titus
Phlm	Philemon
Heb	Hebrews
Jas	James
1–2 Pet	1–2 Peter
1–2–3 John	1–2–3 John
Jude	Jude
Rev	Revelation

CHAPTER 1

THE APPENDICES OF THE BOOK OF JUDGES

COY D. ROPER

In Judges 17–21 are found two unusual groups of stories. Judges 17 tells how a man named Micah established a shrine at his own house, complete with his own Levitical priest and a molten image dedicated to Yahweh. Judges 18 concludes the story by describing how the tribe of Dan secured a territory for itself at Laish, and in the process also secured Micah's image and priest and set up its own sanctuary in its new territory. Judges 19–21 presents another cycle of stories: Judges 19 tells how a Levite whose concubine had left him went to bring her home again, but on the return journey was subjected to terrible discourtesy by the people of Gibeah. His concubine was raped and killed. In Judges 20 and 21 this evil deed is avenged; first, the people of all Israel attack and almost completely destroy Benjamin, because Benjamin has refused to allow the perpetrators of the outrage to be punished; second, the people realize that they have almost wiped out a complete tribe, and so they seek to find ways to provide for a continuation of Benjamin.[1]

The reader of the book of Judges immediately notes a discontinuity between these stories and what has preceded them in the earlier part of the book:[2] (1) The structure of the book of Judges is built around heroes, known as "judges." But there are no such heroes or deliverers in these stories. (2) In the earlier part of Judges these judges deliver Israel, or parts of Israel, from external threats, from the oppression of the nations around Israel. But in Judges 17–21 the fighting is (mostly) internal; civil war, rather than a war of conquest or of defense, is pictured. (3) In the earlier part of Judges, a cyclical pattern is obvious: apostasy, oppression, repentance, deliverance. In this last part of Judges, there is certainly apostasy (although it is not named apostasy), but there is no repentance, no oppression by outsiders, and a very misguided approach to deliverance.

These obvious differences (and perhaps others) have led scholars to separate Judges 17–21 from the remainder of the book and to classify these chapters as appendices.

But just saying that they are different and categorizing them as additions to the book of Judges does not altogether satisfy the reader's curiosity. He still wants to know: Why were they added? How do they relate to the remainder of the book, and to other historical sections of the Old Testament? It is the purpose of this paper to deal with these matters. Specifically, two questions will be discussed: (1) Did the events recorded in Judges 17–21 really occur? (.2) Why were they recorded? What purpose are these narratives intended to serve in their context?

I. THE HISTORICITY OF JUDGES 17–21

Since most commentators distinguish between the two appendices when they address the question of their historical genuineness, the stories of Judges 17–18 and those of Judges 19–21 will be considered separately.

The Historicity of the Migration of Dan

Are the stories told in Judges 17–18 true to historical facts? Most commentators answer, "Yes." Moore says,

> The historical value of these chapters is hardly inferior to that of any in the book. The picture of the social and religious state of the times which they contain is full of life, and bears every mark of truth fulness. ... In this narrative, apart from its own importance for the history of this tribe, we have doubtless a type of many similar enterprises in the period of conquest; cf. esp. Jos. 17:14-18.[3]

In favor of this view, it may be said that the atmosphere that pervades these narratives is thought to be typical of the period; "they reveal the primitive religious ideas and the semi-barbarous manners of the time in a way which convinces us of their value as historical documents."[4] The time, as Bright says, was one of "theological irregularity"[5] and these chapters correctly reflect such a time early in Israel's history. Each area seems to have its own place of worship; there is no temple. Micah makes an image, dedi-

cated to Yahweh, and installs his son as priest. The tribe of
Dan is anxious to establish its own sanctuary with its own
priesthood, so it steals Micah's priest (a Levite whom he
secured to take over from his son) and image. And the
author never comments on the fact that many of the laws
contained in the Pentateuch have been broken. All of this
presupposes a time when religious practices were unortho-
dox, and when such laws as the people were aware of were
"more honored in the breach than in the observance."[6]
Such a time could hardly have occurred at a later stage in
Israel's history.

There is also some archaeological evidence which
makes it plausible to regard these stories as historical. For
instance, Bright says,

> ... the impression one gains-of continual if intermittent
> fighting, with peaceful interludes alternating with times
> of crisis both external and internal--is a thoroughly
> authentic one. It tallies perfectly with archaeological
> evidence, which shows that the twelfth and eleventh cen-
> turies were as disturbed as any in the history of
> Palestine. Most of its towns suffered destruction, some
of them (e.g., Bethel) repeatedly, during this period.[7]

The Historicity of the Outrage at Gibeah

The authenticity of the story told in Judges 19–21 is, in
contrast to the previous two chapters, questioned by many
commentators.[8] Mainly, they give three reasons for their
doubts:

For one thing, the story is thought to have characteristics of fiction or legend. For instance, the numbers appear to be too large. Moore says they are "exaggerated to absurdity."[9] And McKenzie says,

> Here is an evidently much later literary composition. The dependence on other OT material noted above is obvious. In each instance of dependence we have a story composed to fill a gap. We have a large number of glaring improbabilities in the entire account of the war with Benjamin, of which the most glaring is the great losses ascribed to the tribe. The stories of the restoration of Benjamin are each suggestive of fictional composition.[10]

Another reason why the historicity of this story is questioned is that it has such a close parallel to the story of the angels' visit to Lot just before the destruction of Sodom and Gomorrah.[11]

But probably the one thing, more than any other, that in the mind of many scholars argues against the authenticity of the events recorded in Judges 19-21 is the appearance of unity given in these chapters , when they say Israel was not united until a later date. Moore puts the case like this:

> The spontaneous and united action of all Israel is even more surprising than the prodigious numbers. It is perfectly clear from the stories of the judges that there was in this period no union of any kind among the Israelite tribes.[12]

Are these arguments decisive against the genuineness of the events recorded in Judges 19–21?

To reply to their arguments against the historicity of this part of Judges, one might note first that even those who question the reliability of the details in the account admit that there must be some real event back of the record.[13] That is, *something happened,* and the memory of that event lingered. Later scribes may have tacked on details, exaggerated numbers, "improved" the story in various ways, but the incident upon which the story was based, they admit, was a real historical incident.

Also, it could be pointed out that the main argument used against the historicity of the events is itself open to question. The argument says: "Nowhere else in this period of Israel's history is Israel pictured as acting as a united whole. Israel's ability to act together did not come until later, during the period of the kingdom. Therefore, these tales reflect a political development which came much later in Israel's history. Therefore, these tales are not true, but must have been made up." But this argument involves circular reasoning :

(A) We know that Israel never acted as a united whole during the time of the judges, because during that period we have no examples of united action on the part of Israel.

(B) We know that the incident of what appears to be united action on the part of Israel in Judges 19–21 was not really that, because Israel never acted as a united whole during the time of the judges.

Such circular reasoning cannot be accepted as proving beyond any doubt that Israel never acted as a unit during the period of the judges.[14]

As a matter of fact, there is some evidence that at least the majority of the tribes acted together on at least one other occasion--that spoken of in the Song of Deborah.[15] Furthermore, the concept that the twelve tribes were an amphictyony, as held by many scholars, would argue that they had the ability to act in concert.[16]

Does the apparent similarity between Genesis 19 and Judges 19 prove that Judges is not historical? It might prove only that the writer of this part of Judges was dependent on that part of Genesis for certain details in the story, but it would *not* prove that *nothing happened* to provoke the intertribal warfare that followed. And there might be other explanations for the apparent borrowing. One such explanation would be coincidence. Another possible explanation might be that the writer of Judges might have had many stories of actual events to choose from to make his point in Judges 19–21. And he might have deliberately chosen the story that most closely coincided with the story of the destruction of Sodom simply because it *did* provide a parallel to that earlier event. If his aim was to demonstrate the extreme sinfulness of Israel, how could he accomplish that purpose any better than to tell how Gibeah's sinfulness was like that of Sodom?

It would appear, therefore, that the story told in Judges 19–21 is based on an actual incident or on actual incidents, and that it may be more accurate in its details than many scholars have thought. Furthermore, there is no compelling reason to believe that Israel could not have acted together as Judges 20, 21 says they did.

If it is true, as has been concluded in this paper, that Judges 17–21 is, to a great degree, a record of actual historical events, another—perhaps more important—topic remains to be discussed:

II. THE PURPOSE OF JUDGES 17–21

Probably the most obvious question raised by these sections of Judges is simply: Why are they there? Several possibilities have been suggested; each will be mentioned before the one main purpose of the narratives, in the opinion of this researcher, is discussed.

Tribal Memories

One possibility is that these events reflect incidents which were important in the history of certain tribes. The Levites, for instance, are mentioned only in these chapters in the book of Judges. Dan is mentioned eight times in Judges 18, compared with only three notices in previous chapters. Benjamin "scores" four times in the first ten chapters of Judges, and is then named thirty-seven times in chapters 19–21. Perhaps some of these stories were preserved by each of these tribes. Then, as united Israel emerged from the chaos of the period of the judges, specific incidents which were important to particular tribes were incorporated into the history of all Israel. The stories may be included in the book of Judges because they were important to one or more of these tribes.

Explanation of Customs and Situations

It may be that these stories are included in Judges to answer questions like: Why is Dan living where they are? How did there come to be a shrine at Dan? Several specific matters are explained by these chapters:

Conquest and settlement. The migration of Dan may explain how the settlement of actual tribes took place in the land; it may serve as an example of what happened with regard to each of the twelve tribes. It is interesting that Abraham Malamat sees a remarkable resemblance between the Danite migration and the conquest which occurred under Joshua. He discusses ten "essential themes common to both the Danite migration story and that of the Israelites from Egypt":

1. Direct association with Moses or his descendants.
2. Dispatch of spies selected from among the tribal notables, and gathering of intelligence prior to the military campaign.
3. The spies' report and attitude—enthusiastic or pessimistic.
4. The misgivings of the people in reaction to the spies' report.
5. The ethnic character of the campaign, specifically mentioning the non-combatants and cattle accompanying the warriors.
6. The particular number of armed warriors.
7. Oracular consultation, by a Levitic priest, concerning the course of the campaign.

8. Procurement of cult objects while on the move, and their eventual deposition at the final destination of the campaign.

9. Permanence of priesthood secured by a third-generation priest.

10. Renaming of places conquered and resettled by the Israelites.[17]

Malamat says that the tribal episode "is a sort of diminutive model of a campaign of inheritance, which pattern appears on the national scale in the Exodus and pan-Israelite Conquest cycles."[18] It is possible that the person responsible for Judges included this story for that reason: to provide an illustration, and thus an explanation, of the way settlement occurred.

The location of Dan. The stories may have been included also to explain why Dan occupied land in northern Israel, especially when Dan received other territory originally.[19]

The origin of the sanctuary at Dan. Cooke says, "The object of the whole story has been to trace the origin of the famous sanctuary at Dan."[20] If the original Danite sanctuary can be connected in some way with the sanctuary that Jeroboam later built there, and Micah's image can be connected with the calf of gold Jeroboam set up there (1 Kgs 12:26–33), then the explanation would have been even more warmly welcomed by its first readers.[21]

The priority of law over tribal loyalty. Professor Mendenhall, in *The Tenth Generation*, says that the issue in the story of the rape of the Levite's concubine in Judges 19–20 is that "the concern for the enforcement of law and punishment of crime must take precedence over the normal concerns of tribal societies to protect their members at all costs."[22] The story thus illustrates "that the ethic of the new religious community transcends the tendency of tribal groups to protect members who are guilty of gross delicts."[23] The purpose of the narrative, therefore, may be to serve as a kind of "case book" for later generations. Should succeeding ages ever be faced with the question "Which has priority—tribal affiliation or moral law?", this case forever provides the answer.

Illustration of the Evil Character of the Period

The most obvious purpose achieved by these five chapters is that they contribute to the reader's feeling of horror concerning the religious and moral degradation of the period of the judges. Edersheim says, "The first of the two narratives is mainly intended to describe the religious, the second the moral decadence among the tribes of Israel."[24] It should be noticed that both narratives, in the opinion of Edersheim, indicate the decadence of the period. The writer or compiler seems to envision someone asking: "How bad was Israel at that time?" "So bad," he seems to answer, "that, in spite of the law against it, people made images and used them in the worship of Yahweh. So bad that a poor stranger was shown no hospitality by the natives of a city, and his concubine was even raped and killed. So bad that the people of Israel even committed crimes like the sins of the people of Sodom."

It might be well to note that, as Cooke says with regard to the outrage at Gibeah,

[It] seems to have shocked the average sense of right and wrong; but it is important to notice that the real offence, and that which roused general indignation, was the violation of the rights of hospitality. The inhuman conduct of the Levite is passed over without comment; little concern was felt, and no pity is expressed, for the fate of the unhappy woman.[25]

If one wonders how that could be, a modern illustration might help him under stand:

Two American soldiers got drunk and went on a rampage while they were stationed in Japan. They broke into a Japanese home, beat up the man of the house, chased him and his wife from the house, raped the daughter and wrecked the furniture and the building in general. The householder notified the authorities and soon two big burly Military Police arrived on the scene and escorted the two renegades to the stockade.

The day of the court martial arrived and the Japanese householder was called on to testify against the two wrongdoers. The presiding officer requested that the Japanese gentleman explain in his own words just what the two drunken American soldiers had done. The old man stood up and pointed a nervous shaky finger at the defendants. "Those men, those men," he said, "they broke into my house, they came into my house, and they didn't even take off their shoes."[26]

Just as in modern Japan the failure to take off one's

shoes may be a greater crime than the act of raping another's daughter, so in ancient Israel the failure to practice hospitality seems to have been a greater crime than rape and murder.

Polemic Against Later Practices

Another possible reason for the inclusion of these stories in the book of Judges may be that they were inserted as part of an argument against certain practices which were current at that later date.

This point is often made with regards to the establishment of the shrine at Dan. It is thought that the details used in the story told in Judges 17–18 are cleverly chosen and arranged to denigrate the shrine at Dan. After all, that sanctuary was built in a city which was violently and wrongfully overthrown. It was overseen by a priest who could be described as opportunistic and greedy. That priest had been obtained by bribery and extortion. The sanctuary featured an image which had been stolen from its rightful owner. And it had even been paid for in the first place with what had been stolen money![27] "How could anyone worship God," the writer may be saying, "in a place like that?" If this is the case, then it is usually thought that the writer was from the Southern Kingdom, and was a defender of a southern sanctuary—probably that in the Temple.[28]

Another possibility exists, as pointed out in an article by Martin Noth. Noth points out that the narrative has a "pejorative" element, especially affecting the cult image.

The image is not large, not really expensive, made with stolen money, and then it is stolen! The Levite is not treated sympathetically. Why this negative tone? Noth says the polemic is not intended against the royal sanctuary established by Jeroboam. Rather, he concludes "that the polemical narrative of Judges 17–18 stems from the circle of the royal Israelite sanctuary of Dan which was established by Jeroboam I."[29] It was therefore intended to prove that the original Danite sanctuary—which was *not* the same as that established by Jeroboam—was not to be compared with the later royal sanctuary.

Another possible polemic purpose to be found in the last three chapters is that they may be saying something against the kingship of Saul. Burney says,

> Indeed, the conjecture lies near to hand that the whole story of Judg. 19–21 may have taken its rise out of antipathy to the memory of Saul- his native city Gibe'ah, his tribe Benjamin, and the men of Jabesh of Gile'ad who owed him a debt of gratitude (1 Sam. 11) which they were not forgetful to repay to the best of their ability (1 Sam. 31:11ff) being in turn held up to execration by the narrator.[30]

Proof of the Need for a King

The narratives in the appendices also serve to illustrate the need for a king in Israel. That is, in fact, the obvious theme of this portion of Judges, as the text now stands. "There was no king in Israel" is repeated four times in these five chapters, as if this statement is intended to explain why such terrible things could happen. As Moore says,

> The note, "In those days there was no king in Israel, every man did as he pleased" (17:6; 18:1a; cf. 19:1; 21:25), is probably the comment of an editor, who felt it necessary to explain how such lawless doings went unrestrained and unpunished.[31]

It appears, therefore, that the material may have been selected, organized, and edited for the specific purpose of illustrating what chaotic conditions result when there is no king.[32] One might even speculate that, since there apparently *was* a king when those words were written, these stories were used as part of a propaganda campaign to reenforce the king's legitimacy and power.[33]

Another interpretation, however, is possible. The story of Israel's united action in the last two chapters of the book might be regarded as a success, rather than a failure. After all, without an earthly king—with only Yahweh as their king—, the Israelites did punish the evildoers among them, and they did solve the difficult problems that subsequently arose. They acted together, without a king, and so demonstrated that they did *not* need a king. Boling, in the Anchor Bible commentary on Judges, recognizes this fact, although he places the writer and the readers he intends to benefit in the Babylonian exile:

> The reconciliation of Benjamin and the other Israelites was used by the exilic redactor to conclude Judges because it balances the introduction (ch. 1). The

introduction had been tacked on by this exilic redactor specifically to show Israelites living together and with foreigners as stemming from Judah's success in capturing the western hill of Jerusalem (1:8), whereas Benjamin had failed to oust the Jebusites from the old city on the eastern hill (1:21). The redactor in lively narrative form thus reminds discouraged exiles that Israelites had throughout their entire history lived among other nations. He was then able to plead for a united Israel according to the Mosaic ideal, while showing how the loosely organized tribal confederation had become antiquated and been replaced by the monarchy. In his day, he believed, God had dismantled even the monarchy. It was therefore as true as it had ever been that Israelites were men who did what was right as they saw it.[34]

It appears that Boling is saying that the writer (or editor) of whom he speaks is holding up Israel's action and organization without a king as the ideal model for later generations, rather than presenting it as a bad example proving the need for a king.

Illustration of the Potential for a Kingdom

Finally, it appears that the appendices—especially Judges 19–21—serve another purpose also: they provide an example of Israel's ability to act together. The meeting of the tribes to punish the people of Gibeah led to an unhappy state of affairs, of which Israel later repented. Their first decision *may* have been ill-advised, their action misdirected; the reaction to the crime may have been all out of proportion to the crime itself. But it did accomplish this: it showed that the tribes could work *together*. If these chapters illustrate the *need*, they also illustrate the *potential* for a kingdom.[35]

It seems likely that there were two forces at work during this formative stage of Israel's history: centrifugal and centripetal.

The tribes were separated, and were likely to be separated further, by differences in language, culture, and geography. Local shrines contributed to this centrifugal force which divided the people of Yahweh. Bright put it this way:

This situation [not being able to conquer and completely drive out the other inhabitants of Canaan, but having to live among them, or with them separating the various tribes of Israel] conspired with geo graphical factors to set centrifugal forces in operation. The Galilean tribes were separated from their fellows by Canaanite holdings in Esdraelon. Between eastern and western tribes lay the deep Jordan rift. And in the central highlands themselves, where communication is hindered by innumerable lateral valleys, the terrain was such as to abet the formation of little cantons, each with its local customs, traditions, and dialect. We may assume, moreover, that local cults, many of them with patriarchal traditions, exercised a localizing effect on religious life and tended to make the Ark shrine less important, especially to those far away. Local interests quite naturally tended to take precedence over the common good. It is not surprising, therefore, the emergencies that Israel faced being mostly local in character, that the

rally of the clans was usually in direct ratio to the prox-
imity of the danger. Factors such as these serve to
explain the impression of extreme disunity that *The Book
of Judges* conveys. Indeed, but for the spiritual power of
the covenant league with its peculiar institutions, Israel
would scarcely have held together at all.[36]

But there were centripetal forces in operation too,
bringing the tribes together. Smith says,

> The tribes were largely pursuing independent courses,
> though they shared a sense of common heritage and
> were bound by various treaties, or covenants, with one
> another ... the process of consolidation of tribal areas
> and defense against organized enemies gradually pushed
> them toward a more centralized government.[37]

There were heroes who were shared by more than one
tribe. There was a central shrine to which, according to
many scholars, all the tribes owed allegiance and to which
they came at more-or-less regular intervals. There were
attacks from outsiders, which sometimes made it necessary
for tribes to band together for mutual protection. In fact,
it was the Philistine threat which produced the first king.
But another force which bound the people together was
their shared sense of right and wrong, of justice and equity,
and their understanding that evil must be punished. In
other words, it was not only external threats which
brought the people together, but also threats from within
—especially when the threat consisted of a disregard for
the ethical laws which their covenant with Yahweh

required them to observe. In fact, it was this force—their concern for the covenant—which, more than anything else, drew the tribes together. Mendenhall deals at some length with the question of what made Israel one. He notes at one point that "ethnic solidarity is essentially a matter of allegiance to a tradition in a continuity" (p. 11). In the case of Israel's ethnic solidarity: what allegiance did Israel give to what tradition? Israel did not achieve its solidarity through tribalism; rather, "the early faith of Israel consisted historically of a transcending of tribalism" (p. 5). Nor did Israel become one by accepting the culture of the Canaanites; instead "there was a systematic, ethically and religiously based, conscious rejection of many cultural traits of the Late Bronze Age urban and imperial cultures" (p. 12). What furnished the basis for Israel•s unity (and, therefore, for Israel itself)? "Religion furnished the foundation for a unity far beyond anything that had existed before, and the covenant appears to have been the only conceivable instrument through which the unity was brought about and expressed" (p. 16). What was the difficult task set before Israel? "To bring unity to a large and varied population where hostility and intense competition existed before" (p. 19). How was that goal achieved? Israel became one when it became true that "early Israel was the dominion of Yahweh, consisting of all those diverse lineages, clans, individuals, and other social segments that, under the covenant, had accepted the rule of Yahweh and simultaneously had rejected the domination of the various local kings and their tutelary deities—the *baalim*" (p. 28–29). How did this unity achieved through accepting the rule of Yahweh affect a man's relationship with others? "The new concept of religion consisted of man's voluntary submission to the will of God defined in ethical terms that were binding beyond any social or territorial boundary"(p. 25).[39]

It was religion, faith in Yahweh, the acceptance of the covenant, which made Israel one nation.

It is fitting, therefore, that in the last chapters of Judges, it is the ethical requirements of Israel's religion which pulls the people together and leads them as a religious congregation to rise up together to extirpate the evil in their midst.

In fact, in the appendices of Judges, both centrifugal and centripetal forces are at work: chapters 17 and 18 show a new sanctuary set up to provide a further cause for division in the land; chapters 19–21, in contrast, show how an internal emergency resulted in united (though clumsy) action on the part of the whole congregation.[40] It might even be possible to see all of Judges as being a see-sawing battle between powers which would divide and forces which would unite the tribes of Israel. If so, it is significant that the final story included is one in which those tribes act together; unity wins in the end.

If it is the purpose of these final chapters of Judges to show Israel as a potential kingdom—"trembling on the brink" of "kingdomhood"—, then it is easy to see the relationship of these chapters to the book of Samuel.[42] What is implicit in Judges becomes explicit in Samuel. There is a well-documented need for a king in Judges; the book of Samuel puts that need into words. There is the potential for concerted action in Judges; Samuel shows how that potential is finally realized. At first, Israel acts together only very tentatively. Then, with greater confidence and success, Israel goes out as one, as a kingdom, to fight together. It would appear that it is no coincidence that Saul cuts up an ox and sends its pieces around to summon Israel to fight. Rather, he does it because the Levite earlier summoned Israel by the same means.[42] The writer of *Judges* does not borrow from Saul's practice; instead, Saul borrows from the earlier practice of the Levite—which would have been well known, whether or not it had been written down.

All of this means, of course, that this writer does not agree with the majority opinion that the story of Israel's united action in Judges 19–21 must belong to a later period. On the contrary, Israel's concerted action appears to be the most significant fact in the last three chapters of Judges. Israel act together to remove evil from its presence, and so foreshadowed Israel's later ability to act together as a kingdom.

Which of the above purposes best explains why the events recorded in Judges 17–21 have been included in the book of *Judges*? Obviously, this researcher has come out in favor of the last purpose listed. However, it is probably not necessary to choose just one purpose. It is entirely possible that the narratives were intended to accomplish several supplementary objectives.

One final question remains: Do the last five chapters of Judges deserve to be called appendices? If an appendix is thought of as some thing unnecessary, as being merely by-the-way, as something that one can get along as well without, then they surely do not deserve the name. They are rather an important part of the book, and provide a vital link in the history of Israel. Not only do they furnish an explanation and description of a unique period in Israel's history, but they provide a bridge between that period when Israel was struggling to establish itself in the land of Canaan and the time when it became a kingdom. They are part of the "labor pains" of the birth of a nation.

ENDNOTES

1. One problem to be solved is that the Israelites have pledged that none of them will give their daughters in marriage to the Benjaminites. Two things are done to overcome the difficulty presented by this vow; one strategy involves allowing the Benjaminites to carry away maidens at a har vest festival. For parallels to this practice, see Theodor H. Gaster, *Myth, Legend, and Custom in the Old Testament* (New York: Harper & Row, 1969), 444–46.

2. "It is plain that the character and motive of these stories are quite different from those of Deborah, Gideon, Jephthah, or even Samson. They concern themselves entirely with internal affairs, without any reference to oppression or deliverance. Only three persons are mentioned by name in the five chapters. On the other hand, the reader senses the same general atmosphere prevalent in the other chapters of the book." Jacob M. Myers, "The Book of Judges," in *The Intepreter's Bible*, 2 (New York: Abingdon Press, 1953), 798.

3. George Foot Moore, *Judges*, The International Critical Commentary (New York: Charles Scribner's Sons, 1895), 370. Moore also says, "The first version of the story, at least, seems to be very old." (Ibid., 370). Malamat, in discussing the Israelite conduct of war, compares the spy story of Judges 18 with that related to Moses, and concludes that Judges 18 is the more realistic of the two. Abraham Malamat, "Israelite Conduct of War in the Conquest of Canaan According to the Biblical Tradition," *Symposia*, ed. Frank Moore Cross (Cambridge, MA: American Schools of Oriental Research, 1979), 41. Wellhausen

says that Judges 1, 17, 18 "have the best right to be reckoned as belonging to the original stock." Julius Wellhausen, *Prolegomena to the History of Israel* (Edingurgh: Adam and Charles Black, 1885), 233. Concerning the whole of this part of Judges (chapters 17–21) DeWette says, "The passage ... is entirely free from mythology." Wilhelm DeWette, *Introduction to the Old Testament* (Boston: Charles C. Little and James Brown, 1850), 195. On the other hand, Snaith quotes Pedersen as saying that what we have in Judges is "a small remnant of legends which told of the tribal wars and the feats of heroes from the time of the settlement onwards, together with legends concerning the founding of sanctuaries and also stories which are wholly aetiological in origin," and goes on to say, "With much of this we would agree," but "with Albright would say that the course of events was much closer to biblical tradition than the modern aetiological school allows." N. H. Snaith, "The Historical Books," in *The Old Testament and Modern Study*, ed. H. H. Rowley (Oxford: The Clarendon Press, 1951), 95. For a favorable judgment regarding the historicity of the passage, see Charles F. Burney, *The Book of Judges,* The Library of Biblical Studies, ed. Harry M. Orlinsky (New York: Ktav Publishing House, Inc., 1970), 416.

4. George Albert Cooke, *The Book of Judges*, Cambridge Bible for Schools and Colleges (Cambridge: University Press, 1918), xxii–xxiii.

5. John Bright, *A History of Israel,* 2nd ed (London: SCM Press Ltd., 1972), 171. However, Myers notes that in Israel there was "devotion to Yahweh," with the result that "the religion of the period was accordingly virile and dynamic, characterized by enthusiasm and loyalty on the part of the

devotees," that "there was a strong tendency against the use of images of any kind" (with some exceptions), but that morality, especially sexual morality, was low. Myers, 685.

6. To quote an excerpt from *Hamlet.* "The Religious concepts and practices of the Israelites during the period of the judges were extremely diverse and frequently linked with the Canaanite religion." Robert Houston Smith, "The Book of Judges," in *The Interpreter's One-Volume Commentary on the Bible,* ed. Charles M. Laymon (New York: Abingdon Press, 1971), 136.

7. p171. Harrison cites evidence provided by Albright of Greek and Italic amphictyonies which may have been like the social structure of the Hebrews, and notes that Mendenhall has provided parallels among other nations of the kind of covenant arrangement within which Israel existed. He adds, "These secular parallels attest to the antiquity of the covenant solemnized by Joshua, and help to set the conquest and settlement era still more firmly against a background of the Heroic Age." R. K. Harrison, *Introduction to the Old Testament* (Grand Rapids, Michigan: Eerdmans, 1969), 691. In an article Abraham Malamat says, "In passing, we may note that the only renaming of a city in the Bible to which historical credibility is lent by support from external sources is that of Laish/Dan," and then goes on to cite those sources. "The Danite Migration and the Pan Israelite Exodus-Conquest," *Biblica* 51 (1970), 15.

8. For instance, Boling says, ""It is difficult, if not now impossible, to regard these chapters as anything more or less than an exilic narrator's artful elaboration, out of the historical memory and an archaic source recounting the

tragic civil war with Benjamin." Robert G. Boling, "In Those Days There was No King in Israel," in *A Light Unto My Path—OldTestament Studies in Honor of Jacob M. Myers*, ed. Howard N. Bream, Ralph D. Heim, and Carey A. Moore (Philadelphia: Temple University Press, 1974), 43. See also Burney, 456.

9. P. 403.

10. John L. McKenzie, *The World of the Judges* (Englewood Cliffs, N.J.: Prentice-Hall, Inc., 1966), 168.

11. For the parallels between Judges 19 and Genesis 19, see Burney, 444. Boling, in the Anchor Bible, seems to indicate that a literary relationship exists between the two passages because Lot and the Levite are both either called, or operate as, judges in their situations. *Judges*, 279.

12. P. 404. See also Smith, 149; Wellhausen, 237; and John Garstang, *Joshua—Judges* (London: Constable and Co., 1931), 10. Noth, however, treats the tribal association which punished violators as a very real phenomenon. Martin Noth, *The History of Israel* (New York: Harper and Row, 1960), 98, 104, 105. Mendenhall also presumes Israel's ability to meet and act together during this time. George E. Mendenhall, *The Tenth Generation* (Baltimore: The Johns Hopkins University Press, 1973), 29. Smend, though he questions details included in the story told in Judges 19–21, nevertheless does not seem to question the ability of Israel to act together as that passage says they did. Rudolf Smend, *Yahweh War and Tribal Confederation* (New York: Abingdon Press, 1970), p. 34.

13. Moore, for instance, says, "The historical character of ch. 20–21:14 will scarcely be seriously maintained; in the whole description of the war there is hardly a semblance of

reality." But later in the same paragraph he adds, "That this narrative has an historical basis, I see no reason to deny" (405). McKenzie says, "Yet the story of an intertribal war contains nothing improbable in itself … this appears to be a genuine piece of tradition, even though the details of the difficulty have been transformed" (168). Myers says, "These chapters contain basically factual material but are interspersed with embellishments and folkloric motives" (808). Noth is even more positive in his evaluation of the material; he says that the story in Judges 19 and 20 "is certainly based on an old tradition and only appears to have undergone slight literary elaboration" (105). Cooke notes that these narratives "bear obvious marks of antiquity: (a) the account of the outrage ch. xix., and (b) the account of the rape xxi. 15–23 remind us of chs. xvii. and xviii., both by the vivid style of the narrative and by the state of manners and religion which comes to light. On the other hand, (c) the account of the vengeance xx., xxi. 2–14, though parts of ch. xx. are ancient, contradicts what we know from elsewhere about the history of this period." Then he speculates how the "ancient story" was "enlarged and recast" at a later period. But he adds: "There is no reason, however, to doubt that a basis of fact underlies the story" (171,72).

14. In fact, it is possible that Israel's united action in Judges 19–21 represents the one time during this period when the tribes did act together.

15. Kaufmann argues that the judges were *not* merely local heroes, since "at that early time, there was no definite boundary between local and national events. Under certain conditions a famous prophet, seer, or fighter might extend his influence among several or even all of the tribes. A local

distress might become a general one; a local deliverance could be felt as a national one." He then uses Deborah as a case in point; what started as an affair involving only two tribes ended with most of the tribes of Israel being involved. Yehezkel Kaufmann, *The Religion of Israel*, trans. and abridged by Moshe Greenberg (Chicago: The University of Chicago Press, 1960), 257. The Song of Deborah in Judges 5 mentions about eight of the twelve tribes; if all were involved in the deliverance of Israel at that time, as a modern song says, "Two out of three ain't bad."

16. For a description of the amphictyony, see Myers, 685. Orlinsky strongly denies the existence of an amphictyony. He argues, for instance, that the Israelite tribes maintained complete autonomy during the time of the judges, that none of the judges were associated with shrines, that no amphictyonic league ever met at a shrine to select a judge, that there was nothing amphictyonic about the structure of Canaanite society at the time, and that their conception of God as a non-localized deity would not have allowed them to enshrine him in just one place. He does not, however, rule out the possibility that all Israel could, and did, act together in an emergency. Harry M. Orlinsky, *Essays in Biblical Culture and Bible Translation* (New York: Ktav Publishing House, 1974), 66–77. Kaufmann, while not supporting the idea of an amphictyony, says, "Israel had a political organization before the monarchy, though it is difficult to detect because of its excessively 'spiritual' character. It was a confederation of independent tribes whose unity became visible only under certain conditions" (256).

17. *Biblica*, 2.

18. Ibid., 1. Malamat is careful to point out that "far

from indicating any direct connection between the two congeneric stories dealt with in this study, our comparative structural analysis points to the conclusion that they are individual models of different scale, following a basic pattern which had evolved for biblical narratives of campaigns of inheritance" (16).

19. Judges 1:34.

20. Myers says, "The main purpose of the first story in the appendixes is to explain how there came to be a Hebrew sanctuary at Dan and how it was that a Levitical priesthood officiated there" (798). See also C. F. Keil and F. Delitzsch, *Joshua, Judges, Ruth*, Biblical Commentary on the Old Testament (Grand Rapids, Michigan: Eerdmans, 1956), 429, where they say, "The account of the image-worship which Micah established in his house upon the mountains of Ephraim is given in a very brief and condensed form, because it was simply intended as an introduction to the account of the establishment of this image-worship in Laish-Dan in northern Palestine" (170).

21. That there is a connection between Micah's image and Jeroboam's golden calves is assumed by some, but disputed by others. It seems unlikely that Micah's image was the same as that used by Jeroboam, but it may have paved the way for the later image-worship.

22. P. 116, fn. 42.

23. P. 91.

24. Alfred Edersheim, *The Bible History—Old Testament*, 3 (Grand Rapids, Michigan: Eerdmans, 1949), 107. See also Cooke, p. xxxiv, where he speaks of the extreme wickedness of the age, but adds, "... it must not be forgotten that even the rude epoch of the Judges produced its hardy types

of courage and enterprise and reliance on the national God." Keil and Delitzsch also speak of the inclination towards idolatry, which was mixed up "from the very beginning with sin and unright eousness," and of the "deep roots the moral corruptions of the Canaanites had struck among the Israelites at a very early period." But they, too, mention that there was, among the congregation of Israel as a whole, a determination to keep itself pure from corruption (427).

25. P. xxxiv. Another writer says, "The Levite's anger does not arise out of compassion for his abused concubine, for whom he seems to show no personal concern, but out of the feeling that his own dignity and property rights have been violated (vss. 27–29)." Smith, 149.

26 George Gurganus, "Preparation of the Missionary," unpublished mimeographed lecture, Summer Studies in Missions, Abilene Christian College, Abilene, Texas, 1963.

27 Moore says, "Many scholars think that the whole motive is to cast reproach upon the sanctuary of Dan; its venerated image was made of silver which a son had stolen from his own mother; when the money was recovered and dedicated to Yahweh, the greater part of it was kept back by fraud; the idol itself was stolen from its owner by the Danites." He goes on to say, however, that "it is by no means clear ... that the author had any thing of the sort in mind" (370).

28. There are other ideas about what sanctuary is being shown to be invalid. R. Van der Hart argues that Micah's sanctuary was the same as the sanctuary at Shiloh. Then he shows how the story told in Judges 17 and 18 proves that the sanctuary at Shiloh is invalid, because it has no Levit-

ical priest, and the sanctuary at Dan is invalid, because there idols are worshipped. He says, "The material has been deliberately chosen to encourage the recognition of the Davidic monarchy and the supremacy of Jerusalem over all other sanctuaries in the land." R. Van der Hart, "The Camp of Dan and the Camp of Yahweh," *Vetus Testamentum*, 25 (1975), 720–728.

29. Martin Noth, "The Background of Judges 17–18," Pages 68–85 in Bernhard W. Anderson and Walter Harrelson (eds.), *Israel's Prophetic Heritage* (New York: Harper and Brothers, 1962), 81 ,82.

30. P. 447. See also McKenzie, 168.

31. P. 369.

32. "The basic theme of the book is Israel's failure as a theocracy to keep true to the covenant even under the leadership of men chosen of God to deliver them from oppression by the pagan world. The frequent and repeated failures of the twelve tribes to remain true to God and His holy law prepared the way for the institution of a central monarchy." Gleason L. Archer, *A Survey of Old Testament Introduction* (Chicago: Moody Press, 1974), 274. The article on the *Book of Judges* in the *Encyclopaedia Judaica* says, "It would seem that these sections (chapters 17–21) were intended to illustrate the dangers of irregular tribal rule. The potential anarchy could be prevented only by the crowning of a king." Gershon Bacon, "Judges, The Book of," *Encyclopaedia Judaica*, 10 (Jerusalem: Keter Publishing House, 1972), 449. See also: Harrison, 692; Boling, *Judges*, 267.

33. However, Burney notes that the writer may not have been living during the days of a king. He believes, in fact,

that the author of the the words "There was no king in Israel" was an exilic or post-exilic editor who "surveying the course of Israel's past history, may equally well have drawn a distinction between premonarchic and monarchic times, regarding the former in comparison with the latter as an unsettled and disorganized period." (410) At the very least, one must reach the conclusion that the words "in those days there was no king in Israel" were written after there was or had been a king in Israel.

34. *Judges*, 278.

35. Thus, Devaux, in describing the federation of the twelve tribes, during the first stage of Israel's settlement in Canaan, says, "The punishment of the outrage of Gibeah (Judges 19–20) shows us the tribes acting in concert to chastise a particularly odious crime." Devaux is saying: Rather than the rest of the book of Judges proving that Israel could not have acted as one, the incident of Judges 19–21 proves that Israel could, and did, act in con cert. Roland de Vaux, *Ancient Israel* (New York: McGraw-Hill, Inc., 1961), 93. If it is true that the latter part of Judges does indicate a step towards the establishment of a king-dom, it may be regarded as a retrograde step. According to 1 Samuel 8:7, during the period of the judges Israel already had a king! God was their king! When they made a man king, they dethroned God. When that fact is considered, the positive view of the kingship presented in these chap-ters of Judges is remarkable. It is this fact that made Noth remark: "Elsewhere in the entire Old Testament there is hardly a passage which assumes such an absolutely positive attitude toward the institution of the historical kingship." (*Israel's Prophetic Heritage*, 80.) For a discussion of the role

of God as the king of Israel, see Mendenhall, especially chapter one on "Early Israel as the Kingdom of Yahweh," (1–31). Kaufmann speaks of the essentially/theocratic nature of Israel's government before the monarchy in these words: "The tribes do not go the way of their neighbors and establish a monarchy, because they believe simply and strongly that YHWH rules them through his messengers. From Moses to Samuel, apostles of God hold national-political leadership; they represent the kingdom of God, the visible embodiment of God's will in the world" (256). From this it may be argued that since the kingdom of God was already in existence in Israel, any move towards the establishment of a monarchy would be a move towards apostasy.

36. P. 170.

37. P. 136.

38. "The prime factor in the growing national unity was the religion of Yahweh, the God of Israel. The various national and tribal lists, and the tribal relationships them-selves, show that the Israelites were a heterogeneous group held together only by a more or less common experience and by their devotion to Yahweh" Myers, 684–85.

39. *The Tenth Generation.*

40. The "Deuteronomic" editor of the book "shows Israel virtually 'on the ropes' by the end of ch. 1 and painfully but surely reassembled in chs 20 and 21." Boling, *A Life Unto My Path*, 45.

41. The completed work of Judges seems "to have led directly into the stories about Samuel, the last judge." (Smith, 135.) Eissfeldt says, "Furthermore, Sam. shows various connecting links with Judges. On the one hand the

so-called appendices to the book of Judges (chs. xvii–xxi) with their repeated mention of the disasters of the period without a king (xvii, 6; xviii, 1; xix, 1; xxi,25) appear to pave the way for the emergence of the monarchy. On the other hand, Samuel appears, at any rate in a number of narratives, as the last of the judges (I Sam. vii, viii, xii)." Otto Eissfeldt, *The Old Testament—An Introduction*, trans. Peter R. Ackroyd (New York: Harper and Row, 1965), 135.

42. Another writer suggests that the practice may be related to "customs of covenanting" (Smith, 149). See also Keil and Delitzsch, 446. For parallels in other cultures and times, see Gaster, 443–44.

BIBLIOGRAPHY

Anderson, Bernhard W., and Harrelson, Walter (eds.). *Israel's Prophetic Heritage.* New York: Harper and Brothers, 1962.

Archer, Gleason L., Jr. *A Survey of Old Testament Introduction.* Chicago: Moody Press, 1974.

Bacon, Gershon. "Judges, The Book of," *Encyclopaedia Judaica*, Volume 10, 1972, pp. 442–450.

Boling, Robert G. *Judges.* The Anchor Bible. Garden City, New York: Doubleday and Company, Inc., 1975.

Bream, Howard N.; Heim, Ralph D.; and Moore, Carey A. (editors). *A Light Unto My Path—Old Testament Studies in Honor of Jacob M. Myers.* Philadelphia: Temple University Press, 1974.

Bright, John. *A History of Israel.* 2ND ed.; London: SCM Press Ltd., 1972.

BURNEY, CHARLES F. *THE BOOK OF JUDGES AND NOTES ON the Hebrew Text of the of the Books of Kings.* The Library of Biblical Studies, Edited by Harry M. Orlinsky. New York: Ktav Publishing House, 1970.

COOKE, GEORGE ALBERT. *THE BOOK OF JUDGES.* THE Cambridge Bible for Schools and Colleges. Cambridge: University Press, 1918.

CROSS, FRANK MOORE, ED. *SYMPOSIA CELEBRATING THE Seventy-Fifth Anniversary of the Founding of the American Schools of Oriental Research.* Cambridge, MA: American Schools of Oriental Research, 1979.

DE VAUX, ROLAND. *ANCIENT ISRAEL—ITS LIFE AND Institutions.* New York: McGraw-Hill, 1961.

DE WETTE, WILHELM MARTIN LEBERECHT. *Introduction to the Old Testament.* Translated and enlarged by Theodore Parker. Vol. II. Boston: Charles C. Little and James Brown, 1850.

EDERSHEIM, ALFRED. *THE BIBLE HISTORY—OLD Testament.* Two Volume Edition; Volume II. Grand Rapids, MI: Wm. B. Eerdmans Publishing Co., 1949.

EISSFELDT, OTTO. *THE OLD TESTAMENT*. TRANSLATED BY Peter R. Ackroyd; New York: Harper and Row, 1965.

GARSTANG, JOHN. *JOSHUA—JUDGES*. LONDON: Constable and Co., 1931.

GASTER, THEODOR H. *MYTH, LEGEND, AND CUSTOM IN the Old Testament*. New York: Harper and Row, 1969.

GURGANUS, GEORGE. "PREPARATION OF THE MISSIONARY." Unpublished mimeographed lecture; Summer Studies in Missions, Abilene Christian College, Abilene, TX, 1963.

HARRISON, R. K. *INTRODUCTION TO THE OLD TESTAMENT*. Grand Rapids, MI: Eerdmans, 1969.

KAUFMANN, YEHEZKEL. *THE RELIGION OF ISRAEL*. Translated and abridged by Moshe Greenberg. Chicago: The University of Chicago Press, 1960.

KEIL, C. F.; AND DELITZSCH, F. *JOSHUA, JUDGES, RUTH*. Biblical Commentary on the Old Testament. Translated by James Martin; Grand Rapids, MI: Eerdmans, 1956.

LAYMON, CHARLES M. (ED.) *THE INTERPRETER'S ONE-Volume Commentary on the Bible*. New York: Abingdon Press, 1971.

MCKENZIE, JOHN L. *THE WORLD OF THE JUDGES*. Englewood Cliffs, NJ: Prentice Hall, 1966.

MALAMAT, ABRAHAM. "THE DANITE MIGRATION AND the Pan-Israelite Exodus Conquest: A Biblical Narrative Pattern."*Biblica*. 51 (1970): 1–16.

MENDENHALL, GEORGE E. *THE TENTH GENERATION*. Baltimore: The Johns Hopkins University Press, 1973.

MOORE, GEORGE FOOT. *A CRITICAL AND EXEGETICAL Commentary on Judges*. The International Critical Commentary. New York: Charles Scribner's Sons, 1895.

NOTH, MARTIN. *THE HISTORY OF ISRAEL*. 2ND ED.; NEW York: Harper and Row, 1958.

ORLINSKY, HARRY M. *ESSAYS IN BIBLICAL CULTURE AND Bible Translation*. New York: Ktav Publishing House, 1974.

Rowley, H. H. *The Old Testament and Modern Study.* Oxford: The Clarendon Press, 1956.

Srnend, Rudolf. *Yahweh War and Tribal Confederation.* Translated by Max Gray Rogers. New York: Abingdon Press, 1970.

The Interpreter's Bible. Volume II of twelve; New York: Abingdon Press, 1953.

Van der Hart, R. "The Camp of Dan and the Camp of Yahweh." *Vetus Testamentum* 25 (1975), pp. 720–28.

Wellhausen, Julius. *Prolegomena to the History of Israel.* Edinburgh: Adam and Charles Black, 1885.

CHAPTER 2
GOD THE MASTER SERVANT

BILL BAGENTS

From the beginning, the Almighty has demonstrated a servant's heart. Not only did He notice that it was not good that man be alone, He acted to provide a stunningly appropriate companion (Gen 2:18). Even as Adam and Eve were banned from the Garden for their sin, God provided adequate clothing for them (Gen 3:21). When Eve bore Cain, she realized that she had —again—been cared for by God (Gen 4:1). When Cain expressed despair over banishment for his sin and fear of death, God gave him a mark of protection (Gen 4:13–15). What an image! The righteous judge chooses to bless the guilty man who has stained His creation with innocent blood.

Biblical examples of God's loving service to his creatures abound. We think of God's protection of Abraham and Sarah (Gen 12–22). He preserved life during nomadic travels in a hostile land, He multiplied their possessions, and He reaffirmed His gracious promises during a 25-year wait. He even pulled back the curtain to show Abraham future events (Gen 18:16–21).

God had no need to show Jacob the dream of the ladder ascending to heaven (Gen 28). Jacob, on the other hand, had stunning need to meet the God who was protecting and directing him. God's protection of Jacob included the dream of warning given to Laban (31:24, 29). It peaked in the famous wrestling episode of Genesis 32:22–32, where Jacob's ability to defend himself was greatly diminished (his damaged hip), but his confidence in God's protection was greatly enhanced. God repeatedly reached out to Jacob with financial, physical, emotional, and spiritual support.

The Joseph saga is a rich story of promise and providence, of faith and forgiveness. God put Joseph where he needed to be to preserve the lives of His chosen people (Gen 5:19–20). God accomplished for Jacob and his family what they had neither the means nor the foresight to accomplish for themselves.

Bible believers value God's stellar service to Israel during the Exodus. When they had no army, He used the Red Sea to crush their enemies. He led them from Egypt to Canaan on a route of His choice that protected them from early and potentially devastating hostilities (Exod 13:17–18). The Lord served them manna six days a week. Their protein came through the quail He provided. God served them by providing and empowering leaders from Moses and Aaron to Joshua and Caleb. And those blessings continued through the period of the conquest. We particularly note God's encouragement of Joshua in Joshua 1:1–9 and 7:6–15.

Bible believers recognize the cycle of sin-punishment-repentance-deliverance in the book of Judges. Time and again, God gave His people both the deliverer and the deliverance that they needed. He showed amazing grace and the highest level of longsuffering. The story of Gideon stands as a remarkable example of God's patient service while calling a reluctant leader. Though a clear miracle of fire had already established the identity of God's angel (Judg 6:19–24), God still permitted Gideon to request two additional signs (Judg 6:30–40). While we do not recommend testing God in this manner, we take heart in God's willingness to meet Gideon's needs and to help His servant overcome his doubts.

I KINGS 19: A POWERFUL TEST CASE

Few Old Testament examples of God reaching down from Heaven to serve one of His servants can rival 1 Kings 19. Elijah fled in despair when Jezebel ordered his death. He believed that he was alone and that hope was gone (1 Kgs 19:10). In what ways did God serve Elijah?

An angel's touch awakened Elijah. God provided a baked cake and a jar of water (1 Kgs 19:6). After Elijah rested again, there was a second meal accompanied by encouraging words (1 Kgs 19:7–8). God enabled that meal to sustain the prophet for forty days (1 Kgs 19:8). God provided three powerful demonstrations of His power (1 Kgs 19:11–12). He recommissioned Elijah, giving him multiple important assignments (1 Kgs 19:15–16). He promised judgment and justice (1 Kgs 19:17). God corrected Elijah's errant thinking, reminding him of 7,000 additional

faithful men (1 Kgs 19:18). And he gave Elijah a co-worker
(1 Kgs 19:19). It would be difficult to imagine a more well-
rounded and effective set of encouraging actions!

SURPRISING SERVICE

Examples of God's service are not limited to the faithful. 2
Kings 5 recounts God's healing of Naaman the leper. We
remember that this is Naaman the Syrian general whom
God had granted victory over Israel. Naaman's story is
filled with surprising service. The Israeli captive who
served Naaman's wife blessed her captor with word of a
healing prophet in Israel. Naaman's servants blessed
Naaman with bold, wise, and respectful counsel that
helped him overcome his ego and seize God's mercy. The
miraculous healing stands amazing, but so does God's
powerful providential influence. The entire account
emphasizes God's over-arching goodness and documents
God's amazing grace in allowing humans to serve major
roles in His unfolding plan.

Genesis 21:1–21 documents God's gracious service of
Hagar and Ishmael as they had been sent away from Abraham's camp. Their water was gone, and Hagar wept in
anticipatory grief over the coming death of her son. Unless
God had spoken a word of encouragement and opened her
eyes to a nearby well, both would have perished.

Meeting Jonah's need for shade clearly was not God's
primary goal in causing the plant to grow at his camp
outside Nineveh (Jonah 4:7–11). The plant served as both
object lesson and visual aid for the teaching that followed.
God's challenge of Jonah's attitude leads our minds to

Galatians 6:1–2 and the outstanding service of spiritual rescue.

These stories bring to mind the teaching of Jesus from Matthew 5:45, "For he makes his sun rise on the evil and on the good and sends rain on the just and on the unjust." Acts 17:28 applies equally, "In him we live and move and have our being." It is His earth on which we stand and His air that we breathe.

JESUS—THE EMBODIMENT OF GOD'S SERVICE

We love the challenging words of Matthew 20:25–28.

> But Jesus called them to him and said, "You know that the rulers of the Gentiles lord it over them, and their great ones exercise authority over them. It shall not be so among you. But whoever would be great among you must be your servant, and whoever would be first among you must be your slave, even as the Son of Man came not to be served but to serve, and to give his life as a ransom for many.

We love the fact that the God who took on flesh and lived among us always honored those words (John 1:1–18, Phil 2:5–11).

Even before the time had come to begin His public ministry, Jesus rescued a wedding reception at the request of His mother (John 2:1–11). It requires little imagination to realize the embarrassment He prevented. John ensures that we do not miss the more important faith-building aspect of this sign (John 2:11).

Jesus' compassionate service to the multitudes is well documented in the gospels. Matthew 9:35–38 offers compassion as the reason for Jesus' healing and teaching. Matthew 14:13–21 offers compassion as the reason Jesus healed the sick and fed the 5,000. Matthew 15:29–39 documents the compassion of Jesus in healing and feeding 4,000 men in addition to women and children.

Each these examples of divine love and service reflect Psalm 103:13, "As a father shows compassion to his children, so the Lord shows compassion to those who fear him." Jesus embodied the heart and service of His Father (Ps 135:13–14, Isa 63:7).

Matthew 4:23–24 summarizes Jesus' early service to those who were blessed by His presence,

> And he went throughout all Galilee, teaching in their synagogues and proclaiming the gospel of the kingdom and healing every disease and every affliction among the people. So his fame spread throughout all Syria, and they brought him all the sick, those afflicted with various diseases and pains, those oppressed by demons, those having seizures, and paralytics, and he healed them.

Similarly, Luke 7:18–23 reads

> The disciples of John reported all these things to him. And John, calling two of his disciples to him, sent them to the Lord, saying, "Are you the one who is to come, or shall we look for another?" And when the men had come to him, they said, "John the Baptist has sent us to you, saying, 'Are you the one who is to come, or shall we

look for another?'" In that hour he healed many people of diseases and plagues and evil spirits, and on many who were blind he bestowed sight. And he answered them, "Go and tell John what you have seen and heard: the blind receive their sight, the lame walk, lepers are cleansed, and the deaf hear, the dead are raised up, the poor have good news preached to them. And blessed is the one who is not offended by me."

Jesus knew that John would recognize the fulfillment of Isaiah 61:1–2, the very prophesies that Jesus read in the synagogue in Nazareth (Luke 4:16–21). No wonder Peter said of Jesus, "He went about doing good and healing all who were oppressed by the devil, for God was with him" (Acts 10:38)!

With no disrespect to any action of the Lord, we find the service rendered to the exhausted and depleted woman of Mark 5:25–34 and to the widow of Nain particularly moving (Luke 7:11–17). The same can be said of Jesus' decision to touch the leper whom who healed (Mark 1:40–42). Even from the cross under maximum duress, He reached out to meet the needs of His mother (John 19:25–27). Reading beyond verse 27, the text seems to imply that Jesus' work was not finished until He arranged care for Mary—what love!

In perfect congruence with His actions, the teachings of Jesus promoted and honored service. In the judgment scene of Matthew 25, the differentiation between sheep and goats is described in terms of service.

Then the righteous will answer him, saying, 'Lord, when did we see you hungry and feed you, or thirsty and give you drink? And when did we see you a stranger and welcome you, or naked and clothe you? And when did we see you sick or in prison and visit you?' And the King will answer them, "Truly, I say to you, as you did it to one of the least of these my brothers, you did it to me."

The Good Samaritan who loved his neighbor as himself is exemplary because of his compassionate and sacrificial service (Luke 10:25–37). The Good Samaritan sacrificed and put himself at both risk and inconvenient to serve a stranger. Even more importantly, the Good Shepherd sacrificed the prerogatives of divinity (Phil 2:5–11), took on the sins of the world (Isa 53, John 1:29), and gave His life blood for us—while we were His rebellious enemies (Rom 5:6–8). There can be no higher service nor any greater love (John 15:13).

A STUNNING PRE-CROSS ACT OF SERVICE

As Jesus prepared His disciples for His death, He taught what may be the world's most surprising and stellar lessons on service. Through John, the Holy Spirit crafts the story beautifully. "Now before the Feast of the Passover, when Jesus knew that his hour had come to depart out of this world to the Father, having loved his own who were in the world, he loved them to the end" (John 13:1). In full love and self-awareness, knowing that the cross, the denial, and the mass desertion were near, Jesus washed His disciples' feet.

This was neither grandstanding nor manipulation. Physically and culturally, it met the need of the moment. Spiritually, it did much more. It redefined greatness, value, worth, and success in terms of the kingdom of God. It put pride and posturing in their place. It stands as one of the ultimate examples of love over ego. It rejects "rights" in favor of humility.

How wise of Jesus to realize and state that the disciples did not grasp the meaning of His actions in this moment (John 13:12)! Though He made valiant effort to explain (John 13:13–17), many—to this very day—still do not understand. Jesus was not instituting a religious ritual. He was documenting that to follow God is to serve in any and every way that God allows.

GOD'S ONGOING SERVICE

In what ways is God's service to His children ongoing? Three outstanding examples come to mind: prayer, providence, and preparation.

It is amazing to think of God as "on call" 24 x 7 x 365 worldwide from Day One until Jesus returns. He always hears our prayers. In that sense, the faithful are never alone, never forsaken, and never without help. Hebrews 13:5–6 quotes beautifully from Deuteronomy 31 and Psalm 118.

Keep your life free from love of money, and be content with what you have, for he has said, "I will never leave you nor forsake you." So we can confidently say, "The

Lord is my helper; I will not fear; what can man do to me?"

Not only does God always hear the faithful and the seeking, He hears even better than we pray.

Likewise the Spirit helps us in our weakness. For we do not know what to pray for as we ought, but the Spirit himself intercedes for us with groanings too deep for words. And he who searches hearts knows what is the mind of the Spirit, because the Spirit intercedes for the saints according to the will of God. (Rom 8:26–27)

As if that were not sufficiently amazing, Jesus Christ also makes intercession for us from His place at God's right hand (Rom 8:34)! Could we imagine a loving service more precious or more powerful?

And to think that God not only hears our prayers, He answers is ways wiser than our comprehension. And He uses our even our prayers to shape our souls, to form us into the likeness of Christ.

God's providential service to His people is legendary— not in the sense of fictional, but in the sense of wondrous, amazing, and awe-inspiring. Through providence, God got Joseph to Egypt and saved countless lives (Gen 50:20). Through providence God put Esther in place "for such a time as this" to save His people (Esth 4:14). Through providence, Ruth cared for Naomi, Naomi cared for Ruth, Boaz cared for both, and the joy of life was restored. Through providence, God moved Paul out of a deathtrap in

Jerusalem and arranged free transportation to Rome—the city where he longed to preach the gospel (Acts 22–28).

Romans 8:28 strongly indicates God's ongoing providential care for His own. Though they are not authoritative and cannot carry the weight of Scripture, our experiences include blessings—care, service, and protection—from God that can be explained in no other way (Jas 1:17, Prov 3:5–6).

And what of God's service of preparation? Every Christian treasures Jesus' words from John 14:1–4.

> Let not your hearts be troubled. Believe in God; believe also in me. In my Father's house are many rooms. If it were not so, would I have told you that I go to prepare a place for you? And if I go and prepare a place for you, I will come again and will take you to myself, that where I am you may be also. And you know the way to where I am going.

Please pardon the simple and obvious reasoning. The Godhead was able to create the universe in six days. Jesus Christ has had more than 2,000 years to work on the home He will give us in heaven. We find this amazingly encouraging.

Even with the magnificent descriptions of heaven within Revelation (Rev 21–22), we realize something of the challenge of describing spiritual reality in terms that humans can grasp. We view being with God the Father, God the Son, and God the Holy Spirit in a reality of endless perfection and delight as beyond all comprehension. Whatever we dream or imagine, heaven will be better. And the Lord is preparing such a place for us.

AN OBVIOUS, PRACTICAL CONCLUSION

From the beginning, God has served and blessed immeasurably. The Creator has taken care of His creatures at levels that we will never grasp. And He offers us opportunity to reciprocate.

As surely as "we love because He first loved us" (1 John 4:10 and 19), we serve because He first served us. Scripture teaches this truth repeatedly. "For we are his workmanship, created in Christ Jesus for good works, which God prepared beforehand, that we should walk in them" (Eph 2:10).

John 9:4 with Matthew 10:25: "We must work the works of him who sent me while it is day; night is coming, when no one can work," "It is enough for the disciple to be like his teacher, and the servant like his master." We get to be like Jesus. We get to love and serve like Jesus and to His glory.

> Beloved, I urge you as sojourners and exiles to abstain from the passions of the flesh, which wage war against your soul. Keep your conduct among the Gentiles honorable, so that when they speak against you as evildoers, they may see your good deeds and glorify God on the day of visitation (1 Pet 2:11–12).

> For the grace of God has appeared, bringing salvation for all people, training us to renounce ungodliness and worldly

passions, and to live self-controlled, upright, and godly lives in the present age, waiting for our blessed hope, the appearing of the glory of our great God and Savior Jesus Christ, who gave himself for us to redeem us from all lawlessness and to purify for himself a people for his own possession who are zealous for good works (Titus 2:11–14).

God, who first loved and served, calls and empowers us to love and serve. He accepts our service as sacrifices of praise to His name (Heb 13:3, 16). He wills that we continually love and serve as we await the return of His Son. And then He utterly and eternally loves and saves us in His land of perfect rest. Absolutely amazing!

CHAPTER 3

EVANGELISM AND MISSION WORK

A COMPLETE STEP BY STEP GUIDE

TRAVIS HARMON

Step One: Go forth to sow
"Behold, the sower went forth to sow;" Matthew 13:3

One of my favorite passages in all of Scripture is an obscure text in Ecclesiastes 11:6. It says, "In the morning sow thy seed, and in the evening withhold not thine hand: for thou knowest not whether shall prosper, either this or that, or whether they both shall be alike good." I usually think about that verse in the vein of evangelism, and it always reminds me of the parable of the sower. We look at the soil, the seed, or the sower and for whatever reason we become discouraged and withhold our hand. However, we have to remember the sower's job is just to sow.

A few years ago I had to learn this lesson all over again. I was asked to preach in a house church in Ho Chi Minh City, Vietnam. There were about 40 people crammed into a very small living room. Practically every church assembly in Vietnam was illegal at that time but no one seemed to care. I stood up to speak and had a very difficult time communicating the lesson that I wanted to present because of the language barriers, the translator, and my own inability to adequately express my thoughts. Fifteen minutes into my lesson on how we should obey the standards that God has set before us, I became very discouraged. At one point, I actually paused and thought to myself how I was not communicating. I could just see on their faces that I was not getting through and I remember thinking, "I want to quit and just go sit down" but I forged on and completed the lesson.

After the service all of the chairs were moved to face each other and we all ate plain turkey sandwiches and bananas. I met and had a great conversation with the only English speaker present who was not with our group. He was an Englishman named Steve Harrison who had lived in Texas, been a missionary to Australia and had then moved to Vietnam and married. As soon as the meal was over, I had to pack up and travel four hours north to Can Tho to visit another congregation. When I got back to the hotel very late that night I received the following email:

Travis, Terrific to meet you in Saigon (Ho Chi Minh City) and I am especially grateful for the terrific lesson you presented, seriously it cut me to my heart, I am especially thankful to God that my wife Lan and son Khanh, were both moved to study and be baptized, what a fabulous end to an amazing day. I've studied with my wife extensively for the past twelve years, there have been many hours, video's, movies, hand wringing and cajoling. So, Sunday was an incredible day and I must confess I am still in a state of shock, relief, disbelief, but thoroughly amazed and in awe of our God. I look forward to the Possibilities that this presents for the growth of the kingdom in Vietnam.

Thank you for being involved in this marvelous change in my personal circumstances. May God richly bless you.

Steve Harrison

It is *so* difficult for us to remember that the power is not in the messenger; it is in the message. As encouraged as I was on that trip to be able to teach in the preacher training schools in the Philippines and Vietnam and to speak in Singapore, the best work that I was involved in was probably when I thought I was at my worst.

When you are afraid to start because that little voice in your head says, "you don't know enough to do this" or any one of a 10,000 other great reasons you should not even try, or when you become discouraged and that little voice starts to whisper, "give up," then you sow the seed, and withhold not thine hand! Go forth to sow!

Step two: See step one
"Behold, the sower went forth to sow."

CHAPTER 4
SERVING TOGETHER
PARTNERS IN SERVICE TO GOD

DIANNE TAYS

This lesson focuses on three acts we are instructed to perform as Christians to help others see Jesus and to help the Church to grow. They are not the only three things we should be doing but only a start.

First, we are called on to serve others. There are many verses in the Bible that instruct us how to serve others. In I Peter 4:10 we read, "Each one should use whatever gift he has received to serve others, faithfully administering God's grace in its various forms." Ephesians 6:7 continues that thought to "Serve wholeheartedly, as if you were serving the Lord, not men." Luke 6:38 tells us to "Give, and it will be given to you. A good measure, pressed down, shaken together, and running over, will be poured into your lap. For with the measure you use, it will be measured to you." Christ told his twelve apostles in Mark 9:35 that for any of them to be first, they had to be the last and, also, a servant of everyone.

Jesus showed us how to serve others by his example. In John 13:5, Jesus washed the feet of his apostles. Preachers have explained that most people wore sandals or were barefoot in those days. The roads were dusty. A traveler's feet would become dirty. When someone entered a home, a servant would sometimes wash the traveler's feet. By washing their feet, Jesus became the servant to his apostles. Many of us would not be comfortable washing a stranger's feet. Jesus showed us the attitude we should take with others.

Secondly, we are called on to practice hospitality. In Hebrews 13:2 we are told to "not forget to entertain strangers." We are also told that "by so doing some people have entertained angels without knowing it." Peter mentions how we are to practice that hospitality in I Peter 4:9.

We are to offer our hospitality "without grumbling." We are to share with our fellow Christians through our hospitality (Rom 12:13).

Third, we are told to work together for Christ in performing these duties. 1 Corinthians 3:9 states that we are co-workers in God's service. Ecclesiastes 4:9–10 gives more insight on why it is good for us to work together:

> Two are better than one,
>   because they have a good return for their work:
>   If one falls down,
>   his friend can help him up.

We are often presented with ways to serve others in our daily lives or to practice hospitality, yet we do not act on those opportunities. Why is that? Possibly one reason could be that it is hard to follow through with a plan all by ourselves. Ecclesiastes says plainly what can help. Two people are better than one. If one of the two runs into a problem, the other one will be there to help him up. Our Lord knew that it was better to work together. Luke 10 tells us that Jesus "appointed seventy-two others and sent them two by two ahead of him to every town and place where he was about to go." Those of us who have been on mission trips or worked locally in door-to-door campaigns know that it is a lot easier to approach the front door of a stranger if there is a partner with you. Having that partner with you gives you a little more confidence. I was always quiet and shy, but if I was paired with someone else and we approached that door together, I was able to do talk to whomever came to the door.

In the Bible, there are many examples of partners working together to serve the Lord and to help others. A few examples are Paul and Silas; Paul and Barnabas; Peter, James, and John; Mary and Martha; Abraham and Sarah; Moses and Aaron; Joshua and Caleb.

Every person in each of these groups had a strength. On his or her own, each person could have accomplished a good work. As a team, these people were able to strengthen each other and accomplish more work than they possibly could have on their own.

In the Senior Learning Center (grades 5 and 6) at the church I attend, we study the book of Acts over a two-year period. As we study Acts, we learn about one of the teams in the New Testament, the husband-and-wife team of Priscilla and Aquila. We read about Priscilla and Aquila in

Acts 18. Paul is on his second missionary journey and has left Athens for Corinth. As we learn from Acts 18:2–3, Paul meets Aquila and his wife Priscilla. They had left Rome because the Emperor Claudius "had ordered all Jews to leave Rome." We also learn that Paul was a tentmaker. Aquila and Priscilla were also tentmakers. Priscilla, Aquila, and Paul were able to all work together to provide for their own needs. According to Acts 18:18, when Paul left Corinth for Syria, Priscilla and Aquila accompanied him. When they arrived in Ephesus, Paul leaves Priscilla and Aquila. Later in chapter 18 we learn that Aquila and Priscilla met a Jew named Apollos who had come to Ephesus. The Bible tells us Apollos was "a learned man, with a thorough knowledge of the Scriptures." Verse 25 tells us he had been "instructed in the way of the Lord", but he "only knew the baptism of John." Priscilla and Aquila invited him into their home and taught him further. We also know that they opened their home to others. Paul tells us in 1 Corinthians 16:19 that the church met in their house. This couple is an example of serving others, practicing hospitality and being co-workers in teaching others about Christ.

Another team we see in the Old Testament is that of Moses and Aaron. Moses and Aaron show us how partners can have different strengths and weaknesses which they bring to the team. God appointed Moses to lead the children of Israel out of Egypt. Moses was unsure of his ability to lead. He questioned God's choice of him as a leader. In Exodus 3 verse 11 Moses said to God, "Who am I that I should go to Pharaoh and bring the Israelites out of Egypt?" Moses did not think he was capable of speaking. He told God that he spoke with "faltering lips." He also asked God to send someone else. Exodus 4:14–16 tells us that the Lord's anger burned against Moses. The Lord asked Moses

> What about your brother, Aaron the Levite? I know he can speak well. He is already on his way to meet you, and he will be glad to see you. You shall speak to him and put words in his mouth; I will help both of you speak and will teach you what to do. He will speak to the people for you, and it will be as if he were your mouth and as if you were God to him.

The Lord was angry with Moses, but the Lord already had a plan. As we read in verse 14, the Lord told Moses that his brother Aaron was already on his way to meet Moses. God told Moses that he would help them to speak and teach them what to do. The brothers could work together to accomplish what God desired of them. While Moses did not have confidence on his own, he was willing to go to the Israelites together with Aaron. Exodus 7:6 tells us that Moses and Aaron did just as the Lord command-ed them. Something that I noticed as I studied about their team was that whenever we read in Exodus of Pharoah calling for Moses, we notice that he called for Aaron also (Exodus 8:8, 8:25, 9:27, 10:8). As the Israelites leave Egypt, we read that it was Moses and Aaron. As problems arose in the desert, it was Moses and Aaron together dealing with the solution. They work together as a team. When we work together as partners, one person might be the leader but still needs to be willing to accept help from the other partner to help further the work of the church.

We also encounter the team of Mary and Martha in the New Testament. Mary and Martha show us how to practice hospitality in service to God. Luke 10:38 tells us that Martha invited Jesus into her home. Martha was the sister of Mary and Lazarus. We know from John 11:2 that Mary was the one who "poured perfume on the Lord and wiped his feet with her hair." We know also that Jesus raised Lazarus from the dead (John 11:38–43). Jesus apparently had been in their home more than once. He had become close friends with this family as we find out in John 11:5 which reads, "Now Jesus loved Martha and her sister and Lazarus." By inviting Jesus into their home, they were providing hospitality and service to the Son of God. When we invite others into our home, we are following the examples we see in the Bible. We are practicing what we read in Galatians 6:10, "Therefore, as we have opportunity, let us do good to all people, especially to those who belong to the family of believers."

As we read through the New Testament, we see Paul partner with several different people. We see him partner with Barnabas, Silas, Timothy, and Luke as well as others. From these different teams we can learn several things. We can partner with different people to teach others. Paul's first partner is Barnabas. Act 11:26 tells us that Barnabas went to Tarsus, found Paul (called Saul at this point) and they went to Antioch together. They stayed in Antioch a year and taught together. Later Paul and Barnabas go on their first missionary journey together. From something that happened in Acts 15, we learn that sometimes partners have disagreements. It's how we handle the disagreements that count. When Paul and Barnabas were preparing for the second journey, Barnabas wanted to take John Mark, but Paul didn't think that was a good idea. John Mark was with them on the first journey but had left them to return to Jerusalem. Paul and Barnabas decide to go their separate ways. Sometimes we disagree with other members of our team. Disagreements happen but we should be willing to part on friendly terms if necessary. Agree to disagree as long as it is not something contrary to the Word of God. Paul joined with Silas for the second journey. Barnabas took Mark with him. Paul and Barnabas both continued to strengthen the church, just separately. Sometimes we stop our work because of disagreements among ourselves instead of looking for ways to settle the disagreement and continuing to work for the Lord.

Sometimes we do not have a human partner in our work for the Lord, but we always have a partner with us, and that partner is Jesus Christ. Jesus is the best partner we can ever have. We cannot do anything without him. If we are feeling down or unwanted, we should remember that he is with us. If we feel lost and alone with thoughts that no one cares, we should remember that he is with us. He is there through the good and bad. Jesus tells us in Matthew 28:20 "And surely I am with you always, to the very end of the age." It is very important to always keep Christ as the center of our lives, whether we are many working together or one working alone.

Heritage Christian University is made up of several teams working together to further the Lord's work. There are several husband-and-wife teams at HCU. One such team is Pat and Janet Moon. They are a Priscilla and Aquila team, husband and wife working to further the Kingdom of God. They are a great example of Ecclesiastes 4:9–10 that two are better than one. They are both leaders in their own areas of expertise. Mr. Moon is Senior Vice President of Administration. He provides leadership and knowledge to those of us in the Business Office as well as providing information and help needed by any of the other departments. Mrs. Moon is Director of Community Relations. She plans and executes many of the events that take place at Heritage Christian University. Mrs. Moon does it all from decorating our environment to moving furniture and preparing food. Even though Mr. and Mrs. Moon both have their own area of expertise and individual strengths, they are also partners in the work at HCU. On many occasions, when you see one of them working at something, the other is right there beside them helping. They work together on the HCU golf tournament and the Heritage Event. They have worked together improving the landscape on campus, working on the McCreary Cabins, laying flooring, building furniture, and many other projects

Mr. and Mrs. Moon also demonstrate service to others. They practice what was mentioned earlier from Galatians 6:10 of "doing good to all people, especially to those who belong to the family of believers." Hebrews 13:16 tells us "And do not forget to do good and to share with others, for with such sacrifices God is pleased." Pat and Janet work together doing good to others as the Lord has told us to do. On numerous occasions they have prepared meals for someone who is sick or recovering from surgery. They work together to provide the meal, each with their own talent. They very quietly "let their light shine." They don't want or ask for attention. They just do what they know needs to be done. I have worked at several different locations over the years. My years at Heritage Christian University have been my favorite. The biggest reason for that are the people I have opportunity to work closely with every day. Pat and Janet make it easy to come to work each day. Others that I work with further that enjoyment.

When I was little, we used to sing a song in church in which the chorus said to "brighten the corner where you are".[1] Over the years I have remembered the chorus but not the verses. I was reminded of this song when I was looking back through lessons collected from Ladies' Days over the years and came across a poem the speaker had passed out also called "Brighten The Corner Where You Are" by Helen Steiner Rice. I looked up the song I remembered on YouTube and listened to a version performed by Ella Fitzgerald. Both the song and the poem carry the same message. I have included the poem and one stanza of the song below. They are both worth the read.

"Brighten the Corner Where You Are"
by Helen Steiner Rice
From *Poems and Prayers by Helen Steiner Rice*

We cannot all be famous
Or be listed in "Who's Who"
But every person great or small
Has important work to do,
For it's not the big celebrity
In a world of fame and praise,
But it's doing unpretentiously in undistinguished ways
The work that God assigned to us,

Unimportant as it seems,
That makes our task outstanding
And brings reality to dreams
So at the spot God placed you
Begin at once to do
Little things to brighten up
The lives surrounding you,
For if everybody brightened up
The spot on which they're standing
By being more considerate
And a little less demanding,
This dark old world would very soon
Eclipse the "Evening Star"
If everybody Brightened Up
The Corner Where They Are![2]

"Brighten The Corner Where You Are" (song)

Do not wait until some deed of greatness you may do
Do not wait to shed your light afar
To the many duties ever near you now be true
Brighten the corner where you are
Brighten the corner where you are
Brighten the corner where you are
Someone far from harbor you may guide across the bar
Brighten the corner where you are[3]

WE DON'T NEED TO WAIT FOR "SOME DEED OF greatness".[4] We need to realize that God has given us all work to do. Sometimes we think the small things are too unimportant and we let the opportunity to help others pass us by. I have done this at times. I plan to do something but put it off. Later I will say "I meant to send them a card", or "I thought about calling them but it's too late tonight. I'll call tomorrow." Tomorrow I forget again. I don't follow through in my service to others as I should. We should all "be true to the many duties ever near us".[5] We need to take advantage of the opportunities God gives us every day. We never know when "Someone far from harbour we may guide across the bar."[6] We never know who is watching us that we might influence to become a Christian.

Another poem I found in the Ladies' Day material was from *Home Poems* by Kate Louise Wheeler.

"Service"

If you love and trust the Saviour
You can find enough to do;
His good deeds and His compassion
Will be done and felt by you.

His great aims will all be cherished
If with Him you're really one;
Can you think of Christ as idle
While so much remains undone?

His self-sacrificing spirit

Will be exercised by you;
And your faith will aid you ever
While love guides and makes it true.

Faith and love that work together
Will turn drudgery into joy;
And make every service easy
That doth trouble and annoy.

Love will show where service waits you
Tho' it be but word or song;
Faith will prompt you how to do it
Be the service short or long.

You can never be discouraged
While the two together blend;
Joined to faith, love meets all trials
And endureth to the end.

You can leave the lower places,
And mount upward every day;
Winning character exalted
If you faithfully work and pray.

You can reach the best attainments
Doing service that you find;
And a worthier example
You can leave to all mankind.[7]

As Kate Louise Wheeler writes in this poem "If you love and trust the Saviour you can find enough to do."[8] If we look around us every day, we will never run out of things to do. She also writes "Can you think of Christ as idle as so much remains undone?"[9] Jesus was not on this earth a long time and yet the impact He made on all our lives remains over 2000 years later. He tells us in Matthew 9:37 that "the harvest is plentiful, but the workers are few". That should make all of us want to look every day for ways to serve Him and to help others.

Pat and Janet Moon have brightened their corner. Let us all "Brighten The Corner" where we are.

ENDNOTES

1. Fitzgerald, Ella, "Brighten The Corner Where You Are," Lyrics.com/lyric/2081486/Ella+Fitzgerald+Brighten+The+Corner+Where+You+Are.

2. Rice, Helen Steiner. "Brighten the Corner Where You Are," *Poems and Prayers by Helen Steiner Rice*, compiled by Virginia J. Ruchlmann and The Helen Steiner Rice Foundation, Baker Publishing Group, 2004.

3. Fitzgerald, Ella, "Brighten The Corner Where You Are,"Lyrics.com/lyric/2081486/Ella+Fitzgerald+Brighten+The+Corner+Where+You+Are.

4. Fitzgerald, Ella, "Brighten The Corner Where You Are," Lyrics.com/lyric/2081486/Ella+Fitzgerald+Brighten+The+Corner+Where+You+Are.

5. Fitzgerald, Ella, "Brighten The Corner Where You Are," Lyrics.com/lyric/2081486/Ella+Fitzgerald+Brighten+The+Corner+Where+You+Are.

6. Fitzgerald, Ella, "Brighten The Corner Where You

Are," Lyrics.com/lyric/2081486/Ella+Fitzgerald+Brighten+The+Corner+Where+You+Are.

7. Wheeler, Kathy Louise, "Service," *Home Poems*, Telegraph Publishing Co., 1897, pg. 115. [Nook edition] Barnes and Nobles.

8. Wheeler, Kathy Louise, "Service," *Home Poems*, Telegraph Publishing Co., 1897, pg. 115. [Nook edition] Barnes and Noble.

9. Wheeler, Kathy Louise, "Service," *Home Poems*, Telegraph Publishing Co., 1897, pg. 115. [Nook edition] Barnes and Noble.

BIBLIOGRAPHY

Fitzgerald, Ella. "Brighten The Corner Where You Are". Lyrics.com/lyric/2081486/Ella+Fitzgerald+Brighten+The+Corner+Where+You+Are.
Songwriters: Robert Lee Black, Charles Hutchison Gabriel, Ina Duley Ogdon, R Price. Brighten The Corner lyrics © Warner Chappell Music, Inc, Sony/ATV Music Publishing LLC.

RICE, HELEN STEINER. "BRIGHTEN THE CORNER WHERE You Are." *Poems and Prayers by Helen Steiner Rice.* compiled by Virginia J. Ruchlmann and The Helen Steiner Rice Foundation. Baker Publishing Group, 2004.

WHEELER, KATHY LOUISE. "SERVICE." *HOME POEMS.* Telegraph Publishing Co., 1897, [Nook edition] Barnes and Noble.

CHAPTER 5
ACT JUSTLY, LOVE MERCY, AND WALK HUMBLY

A SERMON FROM MICAH 6:6–8

BRAD MCKINNON

I was a first-semester undergraduate student at the University of Memphis in the fall of 1992—nearly 30 years ago now. I was going to class one morning early in the semester when I heard a strange sound in the distance. At first, I couldn't really make out exactly what the sound was. As I got closer, it sounded like it might be someone yelling. The voice seemed deep and intimidating, but I couldn't make out what the individual was saying. As I continued to walk toward the source of the commotion, I topped a hill and could finally see what was happening. There was a man holding a huge banner that resembled an oversized picket sign. The large placard had several scripture references accompanied by warnings of judgment. The man was a street preacher it seemed, and he had chosen us students who were going to class as his audience. He was shouting harsh condemnations as we passed by. He was a large man with a booming voice which added to the intensity of the environment. The whole scene disturbed me, so

I kept my head down and quickly made my way to class. Well, as the semester continued, I noticed the preacher would come back from time to time. I did not know how he chose when to show up, but each time, it was the same routine.

One day I got up enough nerve to approach the gentleman. I recall asking him why he was yelling at me and my fellow students when he really did not know anything about us. How could he know that any of us specifically stood condemned before God or were facing certain judgment? I don't remember what he said in response. All I can recall is that while I was hesitant to approach him, I felt like he needed to be challenged about his method. Why did he feel like this was a valid evangelistic technique? Over the years, I have often thought about this encounter. The more I think about that street preacher's style, the more I have come, not necessarily to think of it as the best approach but to at least appreciate it in a narrow sense. This fellow saw himself as a prophet of sorts and was acting accordingly.

Often when we hear the term prophet, we tend to think almost exclusively about someone who predicts events that are hundreds or even thousands of years in the future. And granted that certainly is a component of a prophet's job description. However, in the biblical text, it seems a prophet's first responsibility was to critique the sins and evils of his or her own day. As Walter Brueggemann puts it, the prophet's goal was to criticize and energize. While there will be an element of "future-telling," prophets "are concerned with the future as it impinges upon the present."[1] This prophetic task of criticizing and energizing was sometimes accomplished through what seems to the modern reader as strange and erratic behavior. For instance, John the Baptist was a prophet, who proclaimed, "Repent, for the kingdom of heaven has come near" (Matt 3:1). What else do we know about John? Well, he wore strange clothes made of camel's hair, and he had a strange diet consisting of locusts and wild honey. He also did strange things. When many Pharisees and Sadducees came out to the Jordan River to be baptized, he responded by calling the group a brood of vipers or den of snakes and demanded they "bear fruit worthy of repentance" (3:7–8). Apparently, he felt they had come to see the show rather than make any true course corrections. As a prophet, John's odd and unexpected behavior helped garner his audience's attention. So, I have come to at least appreciate what a prophet could be—maybe not necessarily the street preacher from my undergraduate days—but at least the notion of a prophet in the biblical tradition.

Quite possibly my favorite Hebrew prophet is Micah. He also had some strange ways about him. I once heard someone say that Micah reminded them of Hoss from the television series *Bonanza*. *Bonanza* (1959–1973) was a western set in the 1860s featuring the wealthy Cartwright family from Nevada. If you are a fan of the show, I imagine Eric 'Hoss' Cartwright played by Dan Blocker is a favorite of yours. The character is based on the timeless Gentle Giant trope. Hoss is a big, barrel-chested guy who's the salt of the earth. He'll always shoot straight with you, and he's unfailingly loyal. Blocker's character became the heart and soul of the series. Those who knew Blocker say that he brought his own real-life happy, friendly, and hopeful attitude to the character he portrayed.[2] Like Hoss, Micah is not from the city. He is a country boy from Moresheth-Gath. Moresheth-Gath was probably located in Israel's Shfela lowland between the Judean Mountains and the Mediterranean Coastal Plain. This area would have been of strategic military and commercial importance (located halfway between Jerusalem and Gaza) and would have maintained a robust connection to the centers of Jewish life. Micah himself, while from one of the provinces, seems to have occupied a position of importance within his community. That he appears not only in his hometown but in Jerusalem as well may indicate he served as a local elder.[3] One of the things that is interesting in the first chapter of the eponymous book is that we see Micah fitting the tradition of a prophet by acting in a bizarre manner. To begin, he says he is going to lament and wail (Mic 1:8). Well, that makes sense. When bad things are happening, we ought to mourn. But then he goes on to say that he will go "barefoot and naked" and will howl like the jackals. To me, this does not sound like an appropriate mission plan, but Micah uses this extreme language to describe how he feels about the problems that existed in the Northern Kingdom of Israel and its capital Samaria, as well as the Southern Kingdom of Judah and its capital Jerusalem.

What is happening among God's people that has gotten Micah so stirred up? In Micah 2 and 3, the prophet addresses three pressing concerns. First, the rich and powerful are taking advantage of the poor and vulnerable. Micah says,

Alas for those who devise wickedness

And evil deeds on their beds!
When the morning dawns, they perform it,
because it is in their power (2:1).

Some people, even if they really want to do evil, do not have the power to do much damage. However, some people have a lot of power and can cause a lot of trouble for others. Micah says the people that had power in his day were causing societal chaos. "They covet fields, and seize them; houses, and take them away; they oppress house-holder and house, people and their inheritance" (2:2). They crave other people's things. Their own prestige and riches are not enough. Rather, they also covet even the little that everyone else has. They want more and more and more, and they are going to do anything, including abuse of power, fraud, and oppression to get what they want. This problem persists in modern societies as well. According to Oxfam, an international public policy organization, in 2015 the combined wealth of the world's 85 richest people was equal to the total wealth of the bottom 50% of the global population.[4] That kind of economic inequality is not sustainable, and it is just the sort of thing that would agitate a prophet like Micah. And I'm afraid the wealth gap has only widened. The situation in Micah's time or in ours does not in any sense correspond with righteousness or what is right. How does the Lord respond? Just like you are devising evil, "I am devising against this family an evil from which you cannot remove your necks" (2:3). They will be "utterly ruined" (2:4).

Second, Micah turns his attention to Israel's political leaders. "Should you not know justice?" he asks (3:1). When the powerful are abusing the weak, leaders should step up to do something about it. They should use their authority to establish justice. However, these leaders "hate the good and love the evil" (3:2). Listen to the colorful language—they strip off the people's skin and eat their flesh. The leaders are eating the people alive. This vivid and disturbing imagery reveals how seriously Micah takes these societal evils. Not much has changed it seems. When politicians go to Washington, they often mysteriously amass great wealth and become people of exorbitant means. Ballotpedia, sponsored by the non-partisan Lucy Burns Institute, has found that between 2004 and 2012, the average American household had an inflation-adjusted increase in their net worth of 3.7%. During that same period, the average increase for members of Congress was 15.4%. And maybe most intriguing, the study found that among Congressional freshmen, from 2011 to 2012, the average increase in net worth in just the first year in office was 8.3%. The study concluded that "the new retirement plan is to get elected and then reelected to Congress and you will be set for life."[5] Public officials gaining wealth for themselves is not a new problem. It was an issue in Micah's day too it seems.

The third group Micah addresses are the "prophets who lead [the] people astray" (3:5). The people's religious leaders should have been guiding them in a way that was right and bringing them closer to God. Instead, they were thinking only of themselves. They cry "peace" when they have something to eat, all the while they were building Jerusalem on bloodshed, wickedness, and bribes (3:10–11). As someone who is from the outside, a good old country boy who is going to shoot straight, Micah steps in to remind the people why the Lord rightly has a controversy with them. Greed, selfishness, and violence have infected the economic, political, and even religious life of the community.

After laying out the indictment, the prophet invites his readers into a courtroom (Micah 6). First, Micah puts on his prophet robes and speaks for the Lord to the people. The Lord calls on the people to answer the charges. "Rise, plead your case before the mountains, and let the hills hear your voice" (6:1). I'm calling as the jury in this case the hills and the mountains and the foundations of the earth. They are always present. They see everything. If you are rich and powerful and you have been oppressing somebody that is weak—maybe nobody even notices—because the weak person does not have a voice. Or you are a politician, and you are taking advantage of your office. Maybe you can cover it up. Or maybe you are a religious leader who tells people only what they want to hear. Maybe you will be popular and attract large crowds. But the Lord says, the hills, the mountains, and the foundations of the earth see everything and hear everything. What is the problem? I have done everything for you, the Lord says. I brought you out of Egypt. I redeemed you from slavery. I gave you good leaders. I have done all this for you. And now you are going to turn your backs on me?

Next, Micah switches places, and he takes on the role of defense attorney speaking on behalf of the accused. Micah's response, especially in verses 6 through 8, is probably the most well-known part of the book that bears his name. Micah asks the Lord a question—what do we do about it? You are right. We are guilty as charged, but what are we supposed to do?

> With what shall I come before the Lord,
>> and bow myself before God on high?
> Shall I come before him with burnt offerings,
>> with calves a year old?
> Will the Lord be pleased with thousands of rams,
>> with ten thousand of rivers of oil?
> Shall I give my firstborn for my transgression,
>> the fruit of my body for the sin of my soul?

What can I bring before the Lord to make things right? Can I come before him with burnt offerings of young calves? Should I just bring more sacrifices? Will that take care of the problem? At first, Micah's response does not really address the abusive or oppressive behavior. Rather, he focuses on external things. Could we just do more religious stuff? Will that make everything right?

Next, Micah intensifies his language. Will the Lord be pleased with thousands of rams or ten thousand rivers of oil? Will multiplying my offerings by the thousands do any good? The implied answer is no. This does not mean that God did not want such offerings. However, simply multiplying these sacrifices without a corresponding change in attitude and behavior would not be sufficient. In the latter part of verse 7, things take a dark turn. If I sacrifice my firstborn child, will that make it right? The implied answer again is emphatically no.

So, what is going to make things right? "He has told you, O mortal, what is good; and what does the Lord require of you." You have already been provided with the answer. As Wolff recognizes, "What Yahweh 'requires' of human beings is therefore nothing other than what he has done for them." Specifically, one is expected to "do justice, and to love kindness, and to walk humbly with God." Stop thinking that participating in a religious activity will make everything okay. Rather, start acting the way God's people are supposed to act toward one another. You cannot be right with God when you are abusing and taking advantage of others. A healthy vertical relationship with God is predicated on a good horizontal relationship with other people. As 1 John 4:20 declares, "for those who do not love a brother or sister whom they have seen, cannot love God whom they have not seen." The reference to the indicted as "mortal" may indicate the kind of responsibility we have to each other as fellow creatures.[6] Before we can walk in fellowship with God, we must recognize the *Imago Dei* in each other. I'm reminded of Ebenezer Scrooge's nephew Fred's description of humanity in Dicken's *A Christmas Carol* as "fellow-passengers to the grave, and not another race of creatures bound on other journeys."

Now go back to Micah 4. In this chapter, there is an interesting discussion about the time when God is going to make everything right. Micah says it will come to pass in the latter days that the mountain of the house of the Lord shall be established as the highest of the mountains and shall be raised up above the hills and people will stream to it. Many nations will say,

> "Come, let us go up to the mountain of the Lord,
>   to the house of the God of Jacob;

that he may teach us his ways

and that we may walk in his paths."

For out of Zion shall go forth instruction,

And the word of the Lord from Jerusalem.

He shall judge between many peoples,

and shall arbitrate between strong nations far away;

they will beat their swords into plowshares,

and their spears into pruning hooks;

nation shall not lift up sword against nation,

neither shall they learn war any more;

but they shall all sit under their own vines and under

their own fig trees,

and no one shall make them afraid;

for the mouth of the Lord of hosts has spoken. (Mic 4:2–4)

Micah envisions a time when God steps into his creation and makes everything right. In essence, the prophet is defining what it means to live a life that is just, loving, and humble. First, it is a life where everyone is welcome. The mountain house of the Lord is going to be established as the highest of the mountains. It is going to be raised up so everyone can see it. The nations and peoples will invite each other to go up to the house of the God of Jacob. We are susceptible to getting caught up in provincial things. We argue presidential politics. We quibble about this policy or that policy. And we forget that when God makes everything right, part of making everything right, will be the creation of an inclusive environment.

Second, he says the nations will beat their swords into

plowshares and their spears into pruning hooks. God is described in Isaiah as the Prince of Peace. When reading about the ministry of Jesus in the Gospels, one thing that emerges is how strange and radical his teachings really sound. "Blessed are the peacemakers, for they will be called children of God" (Matt 5:9). "But I say to you, Do not resist an evildoer. But if anyone strikes you on the right cheek, turn the other also" (Matt 5:39). "But I say to you, Love your enemies and pray for those who persecute you, so that you may be children of your Father in heaven; for he makes his sun rise on the evil and on the good, and sends rain on the righteous and on the unrighteous" (Matt 5:44–45). Unfortunately, even in the church, people can get agitated and upset when they are encouraged to take the teachings of Jesus seriously. Not just quoting a passage here or a passage there but to take what Jesus says and try to live those values out in our lives is truly a challenge. We often fail miserably but just attempting to conform our lives to Jesus's teachings, rather than trying to conform his teachings to our lives, can make such a dramatic difference in our world.

Third, when God steps in and makes everything right, we do not have to be afraid any longer. I was reading a blog recently, and the author observed that fear was not a Christian virtue. I think she's right. Think about those virtue lists we have in the New Testament. For instance, the fruit of the Spirit in Galatians 5. Listed are love, joy, peace, patience, kindness, generosity, faithfulness, gentleness, and self-control. Fear is conspicuously absent. In fact, fear is not found in any such lists in the New Testament. It is easy to give in to fear. It may be real, credible fear or irrational fear we create in our own minds. It's easy to be scared when we don't feel like we have control. An uncertain future can sometimes be overwhelming. And when we get scared, we stop acting in just ways. We stop acting in loving ways. We stop acting in humble ways. We cannot give in to fear.

Finally, consider Micah 5. Except for Micah 6:8, Micah 5:2 is probably the most famous verse in the book: "But you, O Bethlehem of Ephrathah, who are one of the little clans of Judah, from you shall come forth for me one who is to rule in Israel, whose origin is from of old, from ancient days." Gignilliat sees the promise of "a new beginning with a new king from David's line."[7] This new king would be a true shepherd who would "feed his flock in the strength of the Lord" and would provide security and peace "to the ends of the earth" (5:4). You may recall in Matthew's Gospel that the magi or wise men come to worship the King of the Judeans who was recently born. They innocently approach Herod the Great who has been given the same title by the Romans—the foreign occupiers of Judaea. The magi waltz in and inquire of the whereabouts of the new king. Herod's response is one of fear and anger. So, he gathers the scribes together, and he asks where the King of the Judeans was to be born. They say, "Bethlehem, of course! Don't you remember what the prophet Micah said?" Matthew presents Jesus as the new Moses or Israel personified—the Messiah who will make everything right. And Matthew expects the reader to make these connections especially in the early chapters of his Gospel. An evil king wants to determine the location of this special child to destroy him. He tells the magi to find him and report back so he can also worship him. They locate the child. They worship him. They present him with gifts of gold, frankincense, and myrrh. They are warned not to go back to Herod, and so they return home another way. When Herod realizes he has been tricked, he orders all male babies two years old and under to be killed. Matthew knows when his readers read of an evil king who orders the killing of babies, they will naturally connect Jesus's experiences to the story of Moses who as a baby was saved by his mother from another evil king—the Pharaoh in Egypt. Jesus was also protected by his parents as they flee to Egypt. Eventually Joseph is told it is safe to leave Egypt and return home. What does Matthew say? This is just like it is written—"out of Egypt I have called my son" (Matt 2:15; cf. Hos 11:1). He wants his readers to think about when God delivered Israel out of Egypt in the Exodus. Next, when Jesus is about to begin his ministry, he goes through water to begin that ministry. He is baptized like Israel was baptized in the sea to begin their ministry as God's people. Right after Jesus is baptized, he spends forty days in the wilderness, which mirrors Israel's forty-year wanderings in the Sinai desert. When Jesus begins to teach, he lays out what have come to be known as the Beatitudes (Matt 5). There are at least eight or nine blessings in this list. However, if you play with the numbers just a bit, you can get to ten. Just like Moses gave the Israelites the Ten Commandments, Jesus gives his disciples a new Decalogue.

For Matthew, when you see Jesus, you see God's son. You see God in the flesh. You see how things are supposed to be. When you think about how we are supposed to act justly, love mercy, and to walk humbly with God—that's what you see in the person of Jesus. That's why it's so important to get familiar with the ministry of Jesus. To get serious about understanding what living life how he told us to live it really looks like. Because that is what it means to be part of God's people and what God is doing in this world.

So, what do we do with all of this? We could intensify things. And sometimes that may look like the best option. Just go to church more, then everything will be alright, and I can feel secure. The same could be said about prayer and devotional life. I just need to pray more, meditate more, study more. All those outward things are wonderful, but it's not going to take care of the problem. The only way to take care of the problem—the only way to change society —is to begin with ourselves and ask what it would look like if God's people today radically lived out Jesus teachings in our lives. What would that look like for my family? What would that look like for my congregation? What would that look like for my community, my country, and my world? Micah's telling us it starts with us. What does the Lord require? Act justly, love mercy, and walk humbly. Or as Jesus put it, "Whoever wants to become great among you must be your servant" (Matt 20:26, NIV).

ENDNOTES

1. Walter E. Brueggemann, *The Prophetic Imagination* (Minneapolis: Fortress, 2001), 2–3.

2. Jon C. Hopwood, "Dan Blocker," IMDB Mini Biography, https://www.imdb.com/name/nm0088779/bio.

3. Bruce K. Waltke, *A Commentary on Micah* (Grand

Rapids: Eerdmans, 2007), 39; Hans Walter Wolff, *Micah: A Commentary* (Minneapolis: Augsburg, 1990), 6.

4. See "Wealth: Having It All and Wanting More," https://policy-practice.oxfam.org/resources/wealth-having-it-all-and-wanting-more-338125/.

5. "Changes in Net Worth of U.S. Senators and Representatives (Personal Gain Index)," https://ballotpedia.org/Changes_in_Net_Worth_of_U.S._Senators_and_Representatives_(Personal_Gain_Index).

6. Wolff, *Micah*, 180; Delbert R. Hillers, *Micah: A Commentary on the Book of the Prophet Micah* in the Hermeneia Commentary Series (Philadelphia: Fortress, 1984), 79; Charles Dickens, *A Christmas Carol* (1843) *and Other Christmas Books* (London: Oxford University Press, 2006), 12.

7. Mark S. Gignilliat. *Micah* (London: T&T Clark, 2019), 174.

BIBLIOGRAPHY

Brueggemann, Walter E. *The Prophetic Imagination.* Minneapolis: Fortress, 2001.

Dickens, Charles. *A Christmas Carol* (1843) *and Other Christmas Books.* London: Oxford University Press, 2006.

Gignilliat, Mark S. *Micah* (The International Theological Commentary). London: T&T Clark, 2019.

Hillers, Delbert R. *Micah: A Commentary on the Book of the Prophet Micah* (Hermeneia Commentary Series). Philadelphia: Fortress, 1984.

Waltke, Bruce K. *A Commentary on Micah.* Grand Rapids: Eerdmans, 2007.

Wolff, Hans Walter. *Micah: A Commentary.* Minneapolis: Augsburg, 1990.

CHAPTER 6

BIBLE COLLEGE RETENTION
PRACTICE

MICHAEL D. JACKSON

For many years my friend and colleague, Pat Moon, has been a constant source of joy and curiosity in my work in higher education. Pat has served so admirably in his administrative position over various functions of the Bible college, one of which was retention. He was always intensely curious about the matter, and we would often have long discussions about how to adequately assess and understand the retention issue. What follows here is some original research into Bible college retention practice. Much of my curiosity about so many things, including retention, is a direct result of Pat's influence on my life and my thinking. It is a joy to be able to share in some small part in a further understanding of the topic.

Subclassifications with Frequencies and Percentages

Bible colleges may find it useful to know what kinds of retention activities are taking place on campuses that are like their own. Table A1 represents the various specific environmental assessments that were reported by respondent institutions.

Table A1

Environmental Assessments by Institution Size

Retention Activity	ABHE Headcount Quartiles				Total
	25th (n = 27)	50th (n = 14)	75th (n = 10)	100th (n = 11)	n = 62
Environmental Assessments	24 (88.9%)	10 (71.4%)	8 (80%)	10 (90.9%)	52 (83.9%)
Local Surveys	16 (59.3%)	4 (28.6%)	4 (40%)	6 (54.5%)	30 (48.4%)
Noel-Levitz SSI	12 (44.4%)	5 (35.7%)	5 (50%)	6 (54.5%)	28 (45.2%)
CIRP	0 (0%)	1 (7.1%)	0 (0%)	1 (9.1%)	2 (3.2%)
Local Focus Groups	1 (3.7%)	0 (0%)	1 (10%)	0 (0%)	2 (3.2%)
NSSE	0 (0%)	0 (0%)	0 (0%)	1 (9.1%)	1 (1.6%)
CSEQ	1 (3.7%)	0 (0%)	0 (0%)	0 (0%)	1 (1.6%)
ACT Student Opinion Survey	0 (0%)	1 (7.1%)	0 (0%)	0 (0%)	1 (1.6%)

Note. Percentages represent column percentages.

Association for Biblical Higher Education headcount quartiles are included in the chart due to their usage in ABHE's major statistical reports that are sent out to institutions each year. They provide easy comparison points for institutions of various size to determine what specific environmental assessments are in place in similar institutions. The cut values for the ABHE quartiles are 164 for the 25th percentile, 289 for the 50th percentile, and 475 for the 75th percentile. Further subclassification of environmental assessments does not appear necessary due the strong clustering around two major activities, local surveys and the Noel-Levitz SSI instrument. ABHE has long offered consortium pricing on the SSI instrument, which could be the major reason for its extensive usage in Bible colleges (45.2% of respondent institutions).

Table A2 represents specific policies and programs reported by Bible colleges. Several subclassifications are possible with the 23 specific activities that were reported by Bible colleges in the category of policies and programs. The ones used here make most sense to the researcher but are by no means definitive. The value of the subclassifications is that they are a starting point for conversation about how to organize and think about specific retention programs and policies. It is also valuable that they come inductively from the institutional perspective, as all activities reported are reported from observations of the institution's documents that explicitly state that the activities are used for retention.

Table A2

Programs and Policies by Institution Size

Retention Activity	ABHE Headcount Quartiles				Total
	25th ($n = 27$)	50th ($n = 14$)	75th ($n = 10$)	100th ($n = 11$)	$n = 62$
All Programs and Policies	26 (96.3%)	14 (100%)	10 (100%)	11 (100%)	61 (98.4%)
Identification					
Academic Performance Monitoring	14 (51.9%)	5 (35.7%)	6 (60%)	3 (27.3%)	28 (45.2%)
Early Warning System	5 (18.5%)	3 (21.4%)	3 (30%)	1 (9.1%)	12 (19.4%)
Attendance Monitoring	2 (7.4%)	1 (7.1%)	0 (0%)	0 (0%)	3 (4.8%)
Web Form/Software	0 (0%)	1 (7.1%)	0 (0%)	2 (18.2%)	3 (4.8%)
Intent to Complete Survey	0 (0%)	0 (0%)	1 (10%)	0 (0%)	1 (1.6%)
Formal Interviews	1 (3.7%)	0 (0%)	0 (0%)	0 (0%)	1 (1.6%)
Phone Calls	0 (0%)	1 (7.1%)	0 (0%)	0 (0%)	1 (1.6%)
Intervention					
Tutoring	15 (55.6%)	8 (57.1%)	5 (50%)	4 (36.4%)	32 (51.6%)
Counseling	8 (29.6%)	3 (21.4%)	3 (30%)	6 (54.5%)	20 (32.3%)
Financial Assistance	5 (18.5%)	1 (7.1%)	1 (10%)	1 (9.1%)	8 (12.9%)
Course Load Limits	3 (11.1%)	2 (14.3%)	2 (20%)	0 (0%)	7 (11.3%)
Medical Services	0 (0%)	0 (0%)	1 (10%)	0 (0%)	1 (1.6%)
Transition					
Orientation/First-Year Seminar	4 (14.8%)	7 (50%)	4 (40%)	2 (18.2%)	17 (27.4%)
Disability Services	4 (14.8%)	4 (28.6%)	0 (0%)	3 (27.3%)	11 (17.7%)
ESL Support	0 (0%)	1 (7.1%)	0 (0%)	3 (27.3%)	4 (6.5%)
Social Media Community for Distance Learners	0 (0%)	0 (0%)	0 (0%)	1 (9.1%)	1 (1.6%)
Guidance					
Academic Advising	14 (51.9%)	9 (64.3%)	6 (60%)	7 (63.6%)	36 (58.1%)
Mentoring	4 (14.8%)	3 (21.4%)	1 (10%)	1 (9.1%)	9 (14.5%)
Support/Prayer Groups	1 (3.7%)	1 (7.1%)	0 (0%)	2 (18.2%)	4 (6.5%)
Support Centers					
Writing Center/Lab	3 (11.1%)	4 (28.6%)	2 (20%)	2 (18.2%)	11 (17.7%)
Student Success Center	1 (3.7%)	3 (21.4%)	1 (10%)	4 (36.4%)	9 (14.5%)
Remediation					
Remedial Coursework	5 (18.5%)	7 (50%)	4 (40%)	2 (18.2%)	18 (29%)
Comprehensive Services					
Comprehensive Student Success Program	4 (14.8%)	2 (14.3%)	3 (30%)	2 (18.2%)	11 (17.7%)

Note. Percentages represent column percentages.

Accreditation Recommendations and Commendations Related to Retention

In addition to these specific activities, it may be of

interest to Bible colleges to know what sort of recommendations and commendations are commonly given by
visiting teams when evaluating Standard 7d (Retention)
from ABHE's Policy Manual. Since data were available for
the entirety of institutions that responded and agreed to
participate in the study ($n = 70$), these evaluations give a
fuller picture of the needs that Bible colleges have in the
area of retention. In all, 29 recommendations were given to
Bible colleges in their most recent self-study in the area of
retention (Standard 7d). Therefore, 41.4% of all self-studies
contained a recommendation in this area. Without compa-
rable studies of other recommendations, it is difficult to
say how this compares to other standards, but on the
surface, it seems to be a significant number. The majority
of these recommendations (21 out of 29, 72.4%) read virtually identically and are focused on the development of a
comprehensive enrollment management plan that includes
retention as one of its core elements. Six of these recommendations (20.6%) deal with assessment and are encour-
agements to institutions to build assessment of retention
into institutional practice. The remaining two recommendations are simply encouraging institutions to track retention and graduation rates and make them publicly
available.

In terms of commendations, eight were observed in the
respondent group (11.4%). Three of these commendations
were statements of appreciation for institutional commitment to helping at-risk students (37.5%). Two of these
commendations are acknowledgements of institutional
commitment to change (25%). One commendation related
to appreciation for high retention rates. One commenda-

tion related to student involvement in retention efforts. One commendation congratulated an institution for raising admission standards to increase student preparedness for success. It seems that Bible colleges have opportunity for improvement in the development of specific programs and policies related to retention. May the data above provide guidance to this end.

CHAPTER 7

GPS, GOD'S POSITIONING SYSTEM

CORY COLLINS

Trust in the Lord with all your heart and lean not on your own understanding; in all your ways acknowledge Him, and He shall direct your paths. (Prov 3:5, 6)

On the night of July 16, 1999, John F. Kennedy, Jr. took off from Essex County airport in New Jersey in his new, single-engine Piper Saratoga light aircraft into a hazy, moonless night. To fly along the U.S. coast and reach Martha's Vineyard, he would have to fly 200 miles, of which the final phase would put him over the ocean in the dark.

The news of his tragic airplane crash and death not only brought grief to his family; it also created a sense of shock throughout the entire nation. By the time Kennedy knew he was in trouble, it was too late for him to reverse his course. The very idea of his small plane plunging at a rate of 4,700 feet per minute, and 1,100 feet in just 14 seconds, is still staggering and horrifying. Adding to the tragedy was the fact that his wife, Carolyn Bessette Kennedy, and her sister, Lauren Bessette, were flying with him. All three perished.

HOW COULD IT HAVE HAPPENED?

According to the Associated Press,

> the most likely explanation is pilot error caused by two things: disorientation in the night sky and a lack of experience in a swift new plane.
>
> "This wouldn't be the first time a pilot has lost control of a plane because of spatial disorientation or vertigo," said Larry Gross, an aviation professor at Purdue University.
>
> Pilots can become disoriented because their inner ear tricks them into thinking they are level when in fact they are turning. At night or in cloudy skies, there are few visual landmarks to reorient the brain. If a pilot is not trained to use flight instruments, as Kennedy wasn't, he can begin a dive—even a steep one—without realizing it.
>
> "Literally, you lose control of the plane, and you can't determine if you're climbing or descending, turning or flying level," Gross said. Experts view the inky skies, the dark ocean, the mid-summer haze, and the lack of landmarks as a deadly combination that may have sent Kennedy unknowingly into a descent from which he could not recover.[1]

Did you catch that? Kennedy was not trained to use flight instruments. In fact, he had had only about 300 hours of flying experience. Flying a new plane at night, with nothing but water below, he had no visual landmarks with which he could reorient his brain. He became confused. His inner ear tricked him into thinking that he was level when in fact he was beginning a steep dive.

ABC News aviation consultant John Nance reported that spatial disorientation can happen to even the most experienced pilots. "It's the inability of our head to be able to tell us, if we don't have visual cues, whether or not we are right-side up. And it's something that can affect any pilot," Nance said. "Most of us have gotten by with it. John Kennedy didn't."

According to that same ABC News report, federal investigators also said that Kennedy turned down an offer by one of his flying instructors to accompany him that night, saying he "wanted to do it alone." That decision proved to be fatal because the instructor, unlike Kennedy, was licensed to use the instruments.[2]

How sad it is to realize that, from the time he began his flight, there was an instrument on board throughout the flight that could have guided him safely and preserved these lives. An altimeter is an instrument that determines a plane's elevation, its height above sea level. It senses pressure changes that accompany changes in altitude.

Kennedy had never been trained to read his aircraft's altimeter. If he had been, he probably would not have crashed. Instead, he leaned on his own understanding, relying on his own instincts. When his inner ear whispered, "You are level," the altimeter read, "You are going down." However, it was the instrument, not his instinct, that was correct. Because he acted according to what he thought and perceived, rather than trusting the objective truth provided by a reliable source, he lost his life and the lives of those who depended on him. That fatal night illustrates the danger we face if we fail to trust God, the most reliable source of all, to direct our paths in every area of life.

To fly safely, a pilot must trust the plane's instruments, even when they totally contradict his natural instincts.

THE MEANING OF TRUST

To trust is to attach oneself to, confide in, feel safe, be confident, be secure or rely on. It goes beyond the mere acceptance of facts to a deep-seated willingness to live by those facts. Imagine a person seeing a sturdy chair, agreeing that it is strong and steady, but refusing to sit in it. Does that person really trust that chair? Certainly not. It is only when one rests his or her full weight upon the chair that genuine trust has been shown. To trust in is to lean on.

"Trust in the LORD with all your heart" is equivalent to "in all your ways acknowledge Him." One who trusts God recognizes Him, credits Him, and depends upon Him in every aspect of life. "All your ways" would certainly include your worship, but also your work or studies, your family life, your friendships, your language, your entertainment choices and so forth. You are to glorify God in thought, word, and deed, whether on the Internet, on a ball field, on a school assignment, on a church pew, or on a job. Only then does He promise to direct or make straight your paths.

Adam Clarke wrote,

> Begin, continue and end every work, purpose and device, with God. Earnestly pray for His direction at the commencement; look for His continual support in the progress; and so begin and continue that all may terminate in His glory: and then it will certainly be to thy good; for we never honor God without serving ourselves ... Self-sufficiency and self-dependence have been the ruin of mankind ever since the fall of Adam. The grand sin of the human race is their continual endeavor to live independently of God. True religion consists in considering God as the fountain of all good, and expecting all good from Him.[3]

MISPLACED TRUST

One who does not lean on the Lord must lean on someone or something else. One who leans on his own understanding makes himself the final authority, the last word. This was the issue at stake in the first temptation. The serpent asked Eve in Genesis 3:1, "Has God indeed said ...?" He then offered her the opportunity to gain wisdom equal to God and to lean on her own understanding. She took the bait.

Every sin, without exception, results from a person's choice not to trust the instruments (God's objective standards) but to depend on his own instincts, preferences, and wishes instead. The Bible says in James 1:14–15, "But each one is tempted when he is drawn away by his own desires and enticed. Then, when desire has conceived, it gives birth to sin; and sin, when it is full-grown, brings forth death."

The Bible warns us often of the dangers of following our own desires. We read in Jeremiah 10:23, "O Lord, I know the way of man is not in himself; It is not in man who walks to direct his own steps." Proverbs 14:12 notes, "There is a way that seems right to a man, but its end is the way of death." The Lord said through His prophet in Isaiah 55:8–9, "For My thoughts are not your thoughts, nor are your ways My ways," declares the Lord. For as the heavens are higher than the earth, so are My ways higher than your ways and My thoughts than your thoughts."

> For the word of the cross is foolishness to those who are perishing, but to us who are being saved it is the power of God. For it is written, "I WILL DESTROY THE WISDOM OF THE WISE, AND THE CLEVERNESS OF THE CLEVER I WILL SET ASIDE." Where is the wise man? Where is the scribe? Where is the debater of this age? Has not God made foolish the wisdom of the world? For since in the wisdom of God the world through its wisdom did not come to know God, God was well-pleased through the foolishness of the message preached to save those who believe. (1 Cor 1:18–21)

Because the world in its wisdom could not find true

wisdom, God provided His revelation, the message of the cross (1 Cor 1:18).

In what areas must we deliberately choose to trust and acknowledge the Lord, rather than lean on our own understanding? Several crucial ones quickly come to mind, in which we must adhere to God's biblical navigation system, even when—and especially when—it contradicts our own instincts or inclinations. Let us consider some of these vital matters.

TRUTH

Pilate asked Jesus in John 18:38, "What is truth?" People are likewise confused today. Some think that truth is relative, depending on a person's preferences or circumstances. They will say, "This is true for me because it makes sense, because it works, because I like it, or because it feels good." People even speak of "my truth" as distinct from "your truth." Many claim that truth is fluid, determined by the culture, or the majority, or elected officials. Having bought the lie of Darwinian evolution, they insist that truth has also evolved and is still evolving. Surveys indicate that as many as 75 percent of Americans, including many who claim to follow Christ, do not believe in absolute truth. They are leaning on their own understanding, not God's instruments. The child of God agrees with Jesus, who said, "Your Word is truth" (John 17:17). The Christian knows that truth is fixed, immovable and unchanging, because it reflects the perfect character of God.

MORALITY

In the beginning God made one man and one woman, and in marriage they became one flesh. Only at that point did they begin to have sexual relations, as God designed (Gen 2:21–25). Jesus reinforced that original plan and added in Matthew 19:6 (NASB), "Therefore, what God has joined together, let no man separate." No matter how many U.S. states or authorities attempt to redefine marriage in any other terms, they cannot, at least not in any ultimate sense.

No matter how many movies glamorize sexual immorality, it is still evil in the sight of God, as are the other deeds of the flesh (Gal 5:19–21). No matter how many voices declare the homosexual lifestyle to be just an equal alternative, God has declared it sinful (Rom 1:26–27). Human life is sacred and precious in God's sight, even when that human life is still in the mother's womb (Ps 139:13–16). Abortion is the shedding of innocent blood, something that God hates (Prov 6:16–19). No matter how many unborn babies are put to death, God will never declare abortion to be right. We must not allow opinions and feelings to distort the one objective instrument God has given: the Scriptures. Lying, cheating, impure desires, theft, pornography and adultery are just as wrong as they ever were.

People who lean on their own understanding may say, "As long as we love each other, and plan to marry, and don't hurt anyone else, sexual activity is good. A baby isn't in my plan at this time." They ask, "As long as immodest clothing or behavior get me more attention from the opposite sex, what could be wrong with it?" "If it's in the movies, if celebrities are doing it, and if it makes me happy, why shouldn't I do it?" "How could it be wrong, when it feels so right?" One's instincts may say, "You're flying level," but if God's altimeter says, "You're going down fast and hard," it's the instrument that is right.

LOVE

Human instinct tells young people that love is a feeling, a thrill, or a sensation. Love is said to be something you "fall into," "fall out of," or experience "at first sight." Love is thought to be based on chemistry, not a mutual commitment to serve the Lord. Some say, "Love is for me, to see what I can get from you, not the other way around. When the feeling is gone, I can leave you and look for someone else whom I find more interesting." That's the deceptive, dangerous human perception of love.

God's objective instrument defines love as a decision to think and act on behalf of another person, to serve and to give, rather than to demand and take. When we trust in the Lord and lean not on our own understanding, we acknowledge Him by demonstrating these qualities noted in 1 Corinthians 13:4–8a:

> Love suffers long and is kind; love does not envy; love does not parade itself, is not puffed up; does not behave rudely, does not seek its own, is not provoked, thinks no evil; does not rejoice in iniquity, but rejoices in the truth; bears all things, believes all things, hopes all things, endures all things. Love never fails.

We recognize that other people truly love us, or do not love us, in the same way. A person who is possessive, quick-tempered, envious, selfish, arrogant, touchy, or rude does not truly love another person. That is true, even if that first person is cute, smart, athletic, popular, or rich. Even if the chemistry is right, the relationship may be wrong. Even if the romance soars, the relationship may sink. The answer to one basic question must precede all the choices that we make. It is this: Will we lean on our own instincts, or will we take directions from God's objective instrument that cannot fail?

SUCCESS

How do we measure a life well lived? Our culture urges us to seek fortune and fame, beauty and brains. Success is a six-figure income or a six-garage mansion. Our instincts may tell us to do as did the rich farmer, whom Jesus described in Luke 12:13–21. When his land yielded plenti-fully, he was concerned that his small barns were insuffi-cient to store his crops. He decided to pull down those barns and build greater, and there he could store all his crops and his goods. Verses 19–20 let us see his thinking,

> I will say to my soul, "Soul, you have many goods laid up for many years; take your ease; eat, drink, and be merry." But then God said to him, "Fool! This night your soul will be required of you; then whose will those things be which you have provided?"

The farmer had laid up treasure for himself, but he was

not rich toward God. Therefore he was not, in the final analysis, a successful man.

God's instrument defines true success in quite different terms. His Word says that success is found in service and in sacrifice, in giving and in yielding. Jesus defined success in this way in Mark 8:34–38,

> Whoever desires to come after Me, let him deny himself, and take up his cross, and follow Me. For whoever desires to save his life will lose it, but whoever loses his life for My sake and the gospel's will save it. For what will it profit a man if he gains the whole world, and loses his own soul? Or what will a man give in exchange for his soul? For whoever is ashamed of Me and My words in this adulterous and sinful generation, of him the Son of Man also will be ashamed when He comes in the glory of His Father with the holy angels.

Ironically, the One who lived the most successful life in history, Jesus Christ, had no place to lay His head (Luke 9:58). He came, not to be served, but to serve, and to give His life a ransom for many (Mark 10:45). As prophesied in Isaiah 53:2–3, He had

> no form or comeliness; and when we see Him, there is no beauty that we should desire Him. He is despised and rejected by men, a Man of sorrows and acquainted with grief. And we hid, as it were, our faces from Him; He was despised, and we did not esteem Him.

One author has said that we spend our lives climbing

the ladder of success, only to realize, when we reach the top, that we placed it against the wrong wall. If you would be successful in the only sense that matters—the sight of God—aim that ladder toward all that pleases Him. When you reach your destination, you will have no regrets.

JUDGMENT

"It is appointed for men to die once, but after this comes the judgment" (Heb 9:27). God "has fixed a day in which He will judge the world in righteousness" (Acts 17:31). Sinful man, while quite willing to judge those around him, refuses to believe that he himself will be judged. Leaning on his own understanding, he dismisses the wrath of God and the need for repentance and obedience. He may accept the fact that "God is love" (1 John 4:8) but not the fact that "Our God is a consuming fire" (Heb 12:29).

Man's instincts may say that there is no hell, or that it's here on earth. However, Jesus spoke in Matthew 25:41 of "the everlasting fire prepared for the devil and his angels." He called it "outer darkness," with "weeping and gnashing of teeth" (Matt 25:30). He described it as "everlasting punishment" (Matt 25:46).

Man may think, "If there is a heaven, then I and all the people I know are going to be there after we die." However, God's altimeter says in Matthew 7:13–14, "Enter by the narrow gate; for wide is the gate and broad is the way that leads to destruction, and there are many who go in by it. Because narrow is the gate and difficult is the way which leads to life, and there are few who find it." The truth is that, though everyone is invited to follow the Lord and enjoy His blessings, most people will not. They prefer to lean on their own understanding instead.

SALVATION

Because of God's amazing grace, the Bible says, "For while we were still helpless, at the right time Christ died for the ungodly" (Rom 5:6, NASB). Because of the sacrifice of Jesus, sinners can be forgiven. Enemies of God can be reconciled to Him. Every wrong thought, word or deed can be pardoned. Those headed for hell can be spared, redeemed, and delivered. We who have leaned on our own understanding in the past can decide to trust in the Lord with all our hearts and acknowledge Him in all our ways. As a result, He will direct our paths. We cannot save ourselves, but the blood of Christ can save us when we turn to Him as He has directed.

Salvation comes, not from our instincts, but from the gospel.

> For the word of the cross is foolishness to those who are perishing, but to us who are being saved it is the power of God. For it is written, 'I will destroy the wisdom of the wise, and the cleverness of the clever I will set aside.' Where is the wise man? Where is the scribe? Where is the debater of this age? Has not God made foolish the wisdom of the world? For since in the wisdom of God the world through its wisdom did not come to know God, God was well-pleased through the foolishness of the message preached to save those who believe. (1 Cor 1:18–21)

Our salvation from sin cannot be based on our feelings, which are unstable and unreliable. We may be excited and confident about many things, but the only solid ground of Christian assurance is the Word of God. We may feel saved and yet be lost. Our instincts, our preferences, our perspectives, and our consciences may mislead us. Therefore, God has given us an altimeter, an objective analysis of our position and clear directions to follow.

In order to receive God's free gift of eternal life, you must believe that Jesus is both Lord and Christ (Acts 2:36). You must be pricked, convicted of the sin in your life (Acts 2:37). You must confess His name (1 Tim 6:12) and repent and be baptized in the name of Jesus Christ for the forgiveness of your sins (Acts 2:38). You will receive the gift of the Holy Spirit, and He will add you to His church, in which you will work and serve as an active member of His body. Then, as you continue to live by faith and walk in the light, He will direct your paths. You will not crash but land, right where you want to be, at home on the other side with Him.

ENDNOTES

1. "Most Likely Explanation For Crash: Pilot Error -- Instructors Theorize That Kennedy Lost Control Of His Aircraft."
https://archive.seattletimes.com/archive/?date=19990720&slug=2972815
2. "JFK Jr. Refused Flight Instructor's Help,"
https://abcnews.go.com/US/story?id=91890&page=1
3. Adam Clarke, *The Holy Bible with a Commentary and*

Critical Notes, New Edition, vol. 3 (Bellingham, WA: Faith-life Corporation, 2014), 707.

TANYA'S AND MY DEAR FRIENDS, PAT AND JANET MOON, are outstanding servants of God and of Heritage Christian University. As an adjunct instructor at HCU in the early 2000s, I remember attending a holiday dinner on campus. Janet had decorated the room beautifully, as she always does with each event. She transformed my office and many others. Tanya and I have continually admired her kind spirit, warm friendship, and expert skill in everything she does. Pat has frequently encouraged us, not only in helping to give the university financial stability, but in caring personally about the well being of each instructor and staff member. Pat has invested incredible amounts of "sweat equity" in the school, improving the campus in countless ways. I have also been involved with both Pat and Janet in classes offered at HCU. They are two genuine followers of Jesus Christ, a great team for the Lord, and our very special friends.

CORY COLLINS CURRENTLY PREACHES FOR THE KELLER Church of Christ in Keller, Texas. He previously served with Pat and Janet Moon both as an instructor in Bible and Dean of Students at Heritage Christian University and as a minister with the Highland Park Church of Christ.

CHAPTER 8
BETRAYAL AND REVERSAL
A VISION OF THE DIVINE WARRIOR IN OBADIAH

NATHAN B. DAILY

Obadiah is the shortest book in the Hebrew Bible, at only 21 verses, and presents a single oracle from YHWH condemning Edom, a nation on the southeastern border of Judah. The superscription identifies the book as a vision but provides no information about the prophet. The name Obadiah, which means "one who serves/worships YHWH", is shared by twelve persons[1] in the Bible, none of whom can be identified with the prophet. Whereas a variety of dates and compositional history models between the ninth and fifth centuries BCE have been proposed for the book,[2] the references to destruction and captivity (11–14) followed by the eventual restoration of Israel and Judah (19–20) persuade most interpreters to read the book as a response to the Babylonian invasion of Jerusalem in 587 and, thereby, date the book to the exilic or early post-exilic period.

OUTLINE

I. Superscription (1a)

II. AN ORACLE CONCERNING EDOM (1b-21)
   A. Messenger formula and call to battle (1b)
   B. Edom's presumed security (2–7)
   C. Edom and Israel on the Day of YHWH (8–21)

THE MESSAGE OF OBADIAH

Following a superscription and YHWH's call to battle, Obadiah 2–7[3] presents the impending reversal of Edom's status by the hand of the divine warrior. Obadiah alludes to the mountainous region that protects Edom's territory and capital city, Sela, by asserting that Edom's seemingly secure location in the "clefts of the rock (*sela'*)" only appears as high as an eagle that nests among the stars. According to the prophet, Edom's boast that no one can "bring me down (√*yrd*) to earth" is simply self-deception (√*nš'*, 3). In fact, complete destruction is near as trusted neighbors are deceiving (√*nš'*, 7) Edom and the nations are being called to war (1) because YHWH is prepared and able to bring Edom down (√*yrd*) from any height (4). By inciting Edom's own covenant partners and friends to deceive and attack, YHWH engineers the downfall of Edom in terms categorically parallel to Edom's role in Judah's destruction.

The final unit of the oracle announces the destruction of Edom, including the wise, the advisers, and the warriors (8–9). The remainder of the book builds upon 1b–7 by revealing the reason Edom will be punished (10–14) and explaining how this will impact Edom, Judah, Israel, and all nations (15–21). Verses 12–14 contain a series of eight prohibitions that carry the double function of condemning Edom's actions as well as warning any nation who might treat Judah in a similar manner (15).[4] The syntactical construction presents the series of prohibitions as acts that should not happen; yet, in the context of the book of Obadiah the prohibitions are framed as actions that the Edomites have previously undertaken. As each prohibition introduces an element of Judah's suffering, the specification extends beyond command to indictment over kinship betrayal.

The scope of Edom's punishment is highlighted by the twelve occurrences of the word "day" (*yôm*) in verses 8–18. The prophet charges Edom for the disaster, calamity, and destruction Judah experienced "on the day" Jerusalem was destroyed. Edom's guilt is emphasized through the phrase "on the day of their disaster" (*bĕyôm 'êdām*) which sounds much like "on the day of Edom" (*bĕyôm 'ĕdôm*). For mistreating Israel "on that day," Edom can now expect the exact treatment on "the day of YHWH" (8, 15). Conversely, a remnant of Israel can expect not only to repossess (√*yrš* occurs 5 times in 17–20) its land (17) but also to occupy an extended territory, including Edom, Philistia, and Northern Israel, with Mount Zion reconstituted in holiness and YHWH reigning as king (19–21).

OBADIAH, CANON, AND THEOLOGY

Since the book of Obadiah reapplies older prophetic material in a new situation (Jer 49:7–22; cf. Obad 1–7),[5] is itself utilized within the oracles of later prophets (Joel 3:5 [2:32]; 4:17 [3:17]; cf. Obad 18), and contains parallel phrases with many biblical books,[6] readers are presented with multiple opportunities for reflection upon this small book's theological contribution to prominent themes within the biblical canon.

Reading Obadiah alongside other canonical texts aids readers in understanding why the single nation of Edom receives an emphatic condemnation when Babylon, who destroyed Jerusalem in 587, is not mentioned in the book. Animosity and conflict characterize the history of the relationship between Edom and Israel (e.g., Num 20:14–21; 2 Kgs 8:20–24; Isa 63:1–6; Amos 1:11–12; Mal 1), and several biblical texts even allude to Edom's involvement in the destruction of Jerusalem in 587 (Ps 137; Lam 4:21–22; Ezek 25:12–14; 35:2–15; cf. Obad 10–14). Drawing upon the traditions of Jacob and Esau as the eponymous ancestors of Edom and Israel (Gen 25–27) who live in conflict but ultimately reconcile (Gen 25:19–27; 27; 33:1–17), the prophet emphasizes Edom's guilt by making explicit reference to Edom as Esau, the brother of Jacob/Israel (6, 8, 9, 10, 12, 18, 19, 21). Based on this kinship relationship (cf. Deut 23:7–8 [8–9]), Edom had a responsibility to help a family member but now, by joining the enemy in Israel's time of great need, has become an enemy of Israel and YHWH.[7]

In response to the devastation, loss, and suffering experienced in 587, Obadiah presents a vision of YHWH as a sovereign who is intimately concerned with justice in the world. YHWH's allocation of justice revolves around the axiom "just as you did, it will be done to you" (15; cf. Lev 24:16–22; Exod 21:23–25; Deut 19:21). Therefore, on the Day of YHWH the situations of oppressor and oppressed will be reversed. Oppressors who swell with pride (cf. Isa 14:12–16; Ezek 28:17; Amos 6:1–7; Jer 50:32; Prov 11:2; 13:10) and act as if there is no God will be brought down (Obad 3–4) whereas the oppressed will arise (1) in expectation of a new reality (17–21). For exiles, Obadiah's presentation of a God who is concerned with justice offers a hopeful future expectation. Obadiah does not reflect on the possibility of YHWH's absence during exile (cf. Ps 44; 79; Lam 5) but perceives of YHWH as a God who cares for and is carrying out plans on behalf of Israel by fighting as the Divine Warrior.[8] The prophet offers assurance that Israel is special ("my people," 15), will survive this ordeal (17), and will return home (19–20). Ultimately, this future is possible because YHWH, who reigns from Mount Zion, is sovereign over all nations (21; cf. Ps 22:28–29; Isa 2:2–5). Therefore, Israel, even in the direst of circumstances, can envision future restoration and peace because YHWH is a God of justice who is able and willing to act decisively on behalf of those in need.

ENDNOTES

1. See, 1 Kings 18:1–16; Ezra 8:9; Neh 10:6; 12:25; 1 Chron 3:21; 7:3; 8:38; 9:16, 44; 12:10; 27:19; 2 Chron 17:7; 34:2.

2. See, Hans Walter Wolff, *Obadiah and Jonah* (trans. Margaret Kohl; Continental Commentaries; Minneapolis:

Fortress, 1986), 18–19, 21–22; John Barton, *Joel and Obadiah* (Old Testament Library; Louisville: Westminster, 2001), 120–23; Marvin A. Sweeney, *The Twelve Prophets* (2 vols.; Berit Olam; Collegeville: Liturgical, 2000), 1:281–85.

3. On structure see, Sweeney, *The Twelve Prophets*, 1:280–81, 288–89.

4. Johan Renkema, *Obadiah*, (trans. Brian Doyle; Historical Commentary on the Old Testament; Leuven: Peeters, 2003), 172; Paul R. Raabe, *Obadiah* (AB; New York: Doubleday, 1996), 176–78, 188–90.

5. On Obadiah's use of Jeremiah's oracle against Edom see, Sweeney, *The Twelve Prophets*, 281-85.

6. Raabe, *Obadiah*, 31–33, cites parallels between Obadiah and twenty biblical books.

7. Sweeney, *The Twelve Prophets*, 291–93; Ben Zvi, *A Historical-Critical Study of the Book of Obadiah*, 230–46.

8. See Raabe, *Obadiah*, 60; Barton, *Joel and Obadiah*, 127, 158.

BIBLIOGRAPHY

Barton, John. *Joel and Obadiah*. The Old Testament Library. Louisville: Westminster, 2001.

BEN ZVI, EHUD. *A HISTORICAL-CRITICAL STUDY OF THE Book of Obadiah*. Beihefte zur Zeitschrift für die alttestamentliche Wissenschaft 242. New York: Walter de Gruyter, 1996.

GOLDINGAY, JOHN. *HOSEA–MICAH*. BAKER COMMENTARY on the Old Testament Prophetic Books. Grand Rapids: Baker, 2020.

RAABE, PAUL R. *OBADIAH*. ANCHOR BIBLE 24D. NEW York: Doubleday, 1996.

RENKEMA, JOHAN. *OBADIAH*. TRANSLATED BY BRIAN Doyle. Historical Commentary on the Old Testament. Leuven: Peeters, 2003.

SWEENEY, MARVIN A. *THE TWELVE PROPHETS*. 2 VOLS. Berit Olam. Collegeville: Liturgical, 2000.

WOLFF, HANS WALTER. *OBADIAH AND JONAH.* Translated by Margaret Kohl. Continental Commentaries. Minneapolis: Fortress, 1986.

CHAPTER 9
A SICKNESS NOT UNTO DEATH

ED GALLAGHER

And our very Life came down here and bore our death
and killed it by the abundance of his life.

—Augustine, *Confessions* 4.12.19

In the days of his flesh, Jesus offered up prayers and
supplications, with loud cries and tears, to the one who
was able to save him from death, and he was heard
because of his reverent submission.

—Hebrews 5:7

***

J anet and Pat Moon are some of the best people I
know, some of the best Christian examples I've seen.
They are an example to me. I have accumulated a
large debt to them for their many kindnesses toward

me, and I am grateful to have this opportunity to dedicate a devotional essay to them. I hope it provides encouragement to them and to all its readers. And I look forward to many more years of working alongside Janet and Pat. (In other words, don't retire!)

***

"This sickness is not unto death." We love that prognosis. The doctor invites us into his office for a consultation, so already we're a little nervous. He says, "We found something"—words that make our fists clench. We stop breathing, waiting for him to tell us when we're going to die. And then he says, "It's a sickness not unto death." Ah. Exhale. Loosen fists. We can relax a little. But, actually, of course, a doctor wouldn't say something like, "It's not a sickness unto death." He'd say something more like, "There's a ninety percent chance this is not a sickness unto death," or "chances are this is not a sickness unto death." Doctors don't like to speak in certainties; they like to hedge their bets.

But these are the words of Jesus in John 11:4, and Jesus does not hedge his bets. Jesus is always certain. So when he hears that Lazarus is sick, and responds by saying "this sickness is not unto death," we can be sure he knows of what he speaks. Do you know what happens next? Lazarus dies.

That's disappointing. Certainly Martha was disappointed in Jesus. "Lord, if you had been here, my brother would not have died" (v. 21). Certainly Martha's sister Mary was disappointed in Jesus: "Lord, if you had been here, my brother would not have died" (v. 32). They were the ones who had sent a note to Jesus telling him about Lazarus' illness (v. 3).

Jesus sometimes received messages like this. One time a centurion sent a message to Jesus telling him about his sick servant (Matt 8:5–13 // Luke 7:1–10). The Jewish elders sent by this centurion testified about his good deeds, telling Jesus about how this Gentile had shown favor to God's people by building their synagogue. Then the centurion sent a second delegation to explain that he knew how authority works, so he was confident there would be no need for Jesus to come to his house; surely Jesus could get the job done from a distance (Luke 7:6–8). He was right. Jesus healed that servant without stepping foot in the centurion's house, without ever laying eyes on the centurion or the slave, perhaps without ever even knowing their names.

There was another time Jesus did something like that, when a Gentile woman from the region of Tyre and Sidon appealed to Jesus on behalf of her demon-possessed daughter (Matt 15:21–28 // Mark 7:24–30). There was a bit of a back-and-forth between this mother and Jesus, but the result was the same as in the case of the centurion. Jesus simply pronounced the daughter cured without ever seeing her or touching her or saying any kind of magic words. That's the kind of power Jesus has.

So, when Mary and Martha send a message to Jesus telling him that Lazarus is sick (John 11:3), surely in this instance, Jesus would act, and act quickly. After all, this is a family that Jesus knows well. He's been in their house before; he's friends with them, good friends. We actually read about Lazarus only here in the Gospel of John (in ch. 11, and in some later verses in the Gospel), but we read about the sisters Mary and Martha in one other passage, in the Gospel of Luke (10:38–42). That's the passage where Jesus is visiting in their home, and Martha is worried and bothered about so many things, but Mary has chosen the good part, because she's at the feet of Jesus listening to him. This is a family that Jesus knows so well that when Lazarus gets sick, Mary and Martha don't even mention his name; their message to Jesus simply says, "The one whom you love is sick" (John 11:3). They know full well that Jesus will know exactly who they're talking about, and they have every confidence that Jesus will drop everything for his dear friends and come immediately.

And so Jesus does ... nothing. He stays put. He waits. He does not respond to the urgent message of his friends. He does nothing at all.

Note the word "therefore" (or "accordingly" or "so," depending on your translation) in John 11:5–6. Because Jesus loved this family, he waited.

LAZARUS IS ASLEEP

After a few days, Jesus tells his disciples that Lazarus has fallen asleep (v. 11). Of course, Jesus means he's died, but the disciples don't get it, and so he has to be more explicit with them: "Lazarus is dead" (v. 14). But at first he described Lazarus' death as sleep. That's reminiscent of the story about Jairus and his daughter (Matt 9:18–26 // Mark 5:21–43 // Luke 8:40–56). When Jesus arrived at Jairus' house and found all those people mourning the death of this young girl, Jesus told them, "She's not dead but asleep" (Mark 5:39). Of course, she was dead, she was not asleep. That's why the people who heard Jesus laughed at him as a fool (Mark 5:40). They had checked her pulse: nothing. They had seen that she wasn't breathing. We can be confident that her heart had stopped beating and her brain activity had ceased. She was dead. So, why would Jesus say she was sleeping?

Sometimes in the morning I have to go to my kids' rooms and wake them up. I'll go into my sons' room, and hardly ever do I have to get my son Marvin up, but Josiah maybe. I'll say, "Josiah, get up. It's time to get ready for the day." Or in my daughters' room, it's not infrequent that I'll have to get Evelyn up. "Evelyn, get up and get dressed. Start doing your chore." I'll call out their names and tell them to get up. That's all it takes. Well, sort of. I'll have to do it a few times. But that's what Jesus means. She may have been dead to everyone else, but to Jesus she was just asleep, because all he had to do was to say, "Little girl, get up," and she got up (Mark 5:41–42).

The Bible often represents death as a type of sleep.[2] When the first martyr, Stephen, was being stoned to death in Acts 7, after he had prayed, the text says "he fell asleep" (v. 60). That's sort of a funny image, isn't it? He's being pelted with stones, and he falls asleep? Of course, what it means is that he died. The Bible I use regularly (the NRSV) thinks it sounds a little too funny, so they actually put in the text "he died," and then in the note they admit that literally the Greek says "he fell asleep." It's the same sort of thing when Paul says, "we shall not all sleep, but we shall all be changed" (1 Cor 15:51); he means that we won't all die, some of us will be alive when Jesus returns and the big transformation happens. Or there's that other passage, when Paul says that at the return of Jesus, those of us who are alive will not precede those who sleep (1 Thess 4:15). Again, he's talking about dead people. The Bible frequently uses the metaphor of sleep to refer to death. In the Old Testament there are all kinds of references to people who have died as "sleeping with their fathers" (e.g., 1 Kings 11:43; 14:20; etc.). The Talmud describes sleep as a partial death: "Sleep is one-sixtieth of death."[3]

Why is that? What do sleep and death have in common? You can probably think of several similarities that I haven't thought about, but I think at least two similarities make a lot of sense. First of all, sleep is restful, and for that reason it is precious. We long for rest; we desire it. Sleep can be hard to come by. As I write this, my family has a new baby in the house, for the first time in about a decade. There's the saying, "sleep like a baby," and sometimes people turn that into a joke: "I sleep like a baby. I wake up every few hours screaming." Well, that is how a baby sleeps, but of course the saying refers to the fact that a baby can sleep through anything. In the middle of the day, with all kinds of noises around, a baby will sleep right through it all. I myself do not sleep like a baby in that sense. I've now started my fifth decade of life, and sleep is harder and harder to come by. Conditions have to be close to perfect for me to get a good sleep. I need white noise, but a particular type of white noise, created by a little fan. And I need complete darkness. And if anybody is moving in the room, I can't go to sleep. For me, sleep is precious because it's hard to come by. Especially now that we have a baby in the house again, sleep is harder to come by, and that makes it precious. We enjoy that rest when we get it. So also death. The Bible represents death as a type of sleep because death (for the righteous) is peaceful and restful. One ancient Jewish text says that those righteous who have died are in the hand of God (Wisdom of Solomon 3:1). The Gospel of Luke represents the righteous dead as in Abraham's bosom (Luke 16:22). Death is restful, like sleep.

Another way that death is like sleep is that it is temporary. It's not a permanent situation. We tend to think of it as permanent, but the one who has the power over life and death knows that it is very temporary.

That's what Jesus means that this sickness that Lazarus has contracted is not unto death. It will do no permanent damage. After all, this Jesus had earlier said in John's Gospel, "Truly I tell you, anyone who hears my word and believes him who sent me has eternal life, and does not come under judgment, but has passed from death to life" (5:24). And a little later, Jesus said, "Anyone who hears my words will never see death" (8:51).

In our eyes, Lazarus is dead. But Jesus knows he's just asleep, temporarily enjoying a rest.

JESUS LET HIM DIE

Mary and Martha sent an urgent message to Jesus, and Jesus did nothing in response. He waited. He took his time. Mary and Martha were urgent, but Jesus wasn't.

It reminds me again of Jairus. Surely Jairus was very impatient with Jesus. I can imagine when that woman with the hemorrhage stopped Jesus, and Jesus took his time with her, Jairus must have been tapping his foot and looking at his watch and sighing audibly. Probably he said to Jesus, "Come on, we don't have time for this. My little girl needs us now!" I have no doubt that Jairus was feeling the pressure of time. Jesus was not. He was content to go slow. And he went so slow that while he was interacting with this hemorrhaging woman, the message came that Jairus needn't bother with the Teacher any longer, because the girl had died (Mark 5:35). She died because Jesus was so slow. Jesus let her die.

God sometimes lets people die.

Recently I went to the hospital with some other people from church to deliver gift bags to patients and family members in waiting rooms. I went in to some hospital rooms and talked to the people laid up in bed. One lady, maybe my age or a little younger, was happy for a visitor. She had been in that hospital bed for a week with an infection. She showed me how swollen she was. Before that she had been in another hospital in a different city to run some tests and do some procedures for which our local hospital wasn't equipped. So she'd been away from home for a while. Her husband was keeping their autistic son, and of course Mama does most of the work at home, so the husband was struggling. He didn't know how to help his kid through homework, so while the mama was in the hospital out-of-state, they would videochat so she could help the son with homework. I asked her how long she would be in the hospital. She didn't know; she had heard no sort of timetable. I asked if I could pray for her. She welcomed it. So I prayed that God would bless her and her family, that he would be good to them in this situation, and

I prayed that God would heal her. I don't know what God will do. I know that James says we should pray without doubting (1:6), and I don't doubt that God will do the best thing in the situation, but I doubt that I know what the best thing is. I do know this: sometimes God lets people die.

I went into another room, and found an older couple, maybe in their seventies. The man was in the bed, unconscious. The wife was on the couch catching a nap, but she was happy when someone from a church walked in. She told me about her husband, about his heart condition. And she asked me to pray for them. Again, I prayed for comfort and for healing. But I couldn't offer any assurances of recovery. I couldn't tell this woman that her husband's sickness was not unto death. I wasn't sure what God would do.

We have been trained to think that the clock is everything. We have seen enough doctors shows on television to know how this works, or we've experienced it in hospitals for ourselves. There's only limited time to save a life. I grew up with the show *ER*, and I saw scene after scene of someone bleeding out or unconscious or suffering in some other way, being wheeled into the ER on a gurney. And sometimes the doctor would climb up onto the gurney and straddle the patient and beat on the person's chest. People were running around and everybody was yelling "STAT!" We know that if a person's life is going to be saved, time is of the essence. We've seen the monitors with those spiky lines and the constant beep, beep, beep. And we know that if ever that line goes flat, and that beep stops beeping, becoming merely one long note, everything's over. That's it. The person has died, and that's all there is to it. There's no coming back from the dead. It's permanent. We've even seen (how many times?) on TV when the doctor has promised that he's not going to let this patient die, so the doctor is doing chest compressions or some other procedure, furiously attempting to ensure survival over which he has no control, and when the monitor displays that flatline and the beep becomes one solid note, the doctor keeps working on the patient until finally his colleagues convince him that there's no use. When you're talking life and death, time matters. You've got to be urgent.

But in John 11, when Jesus hears about Lazarus, he displays no urgency at all. Martha and Mary are urgent, but not Jesus. Same for the Jairus story. Jesus takes his time. He doesn't realize that time is so all-important when it comes to saving lives. Because, as it turns out, time doesn't matter to Jesus at all.

Death is no impediment to the saving call of Jesus.

It doesn't matter if Jairus' daughter's heart has stopped beating. Jesus just needs to wake her up. It doesn't matter if Lazarus has been dead so long he stinketh. Jesus just needs to call, "Lazarus, come forth!"

God sometimes lets people die because death does not stand in the way of God.

Just like Martha (John 11:21) and Mary (v. 32), there were some other people there in Bethany mourning the death of Lazarus, who also thought that Jesus could have prevented that death if only he had been there (v. 37). This is a faithful response, but it also displays imperfect faith, because it does not acknowledge that Jesus controls life and death. He created life (John 1:1–4), and there is no time limit on Jesus's ability to confer life. After all, "just as the Father has life in himself, so he has granted the Son to have life in himself" (5:26). Jesus told Martha, "I am the resurrection and the life" (11:25).

In John 10:10, Jesus says that he has come to distribute life to people, and he specifies: "a life more abundant." We have been misled by our American culture into thinking that what Jesus came to deliver to us is equivalent to the American Dream. (Some preachers on TV have contributed to this error.) We often think that the abundant life Jesus wants for us is basically Life, Liberty, and the Pursuit of Happiness. He wants us healthy, wealthy, and wise. The New Living Translation actually renders John 10:10, "a rich and satisfying life."

This is all wrong. Remember that Jesus is the one who has life in himself, so that he can distribute life to whomever he will. Right before Jesus says that the Father has granted him to have life in himself, he says, "the dead will hear the voice of the Son of God, and those who hear will live" (5:25). This is abundant life—life so abundant that not even death can overcome it. Jesus has come to so fill us with life that it carries over even into death—nay, rather, it continually increases even in death.

Death is simply sleep. It is temporary and restful. As the poet says, "One short sleep past, we wake eternally and death shall be no more." That doesn't dull the pain that we feel when loved ones die. Well, it should dull the pain a little. And Jesus knows about the pain that death brings. "You will be sorrowful, but your sorrow will be turned into joy" (John 16:20).

Death is all around us. It seems like we hear about some new cause of cancer every other day, or some new shooting, or some natural disaster. Life itself is going to kill us. And we can't control it.

The assurance Jesus gave in the case of Lazarus, he gives to us all. It doesn't matter what the doctor says. That prognosis is irrelevant. Jesus gives us our prognosis.

This sickness is not unto death.

"Son of Adam," said Aslan, "go into that thicket and pluck the thorn that you will find there, and bring it to me."

Eustace obeyed. The thorn was a foot long and sharp as a rapier.

"Drive it into my paw, Son of Adam," said Aslan, holding up his right fore-paw and spreading out the great pad toward Eustace.

"Must I?" said Eustace.

"Yes," said Aslan.

Then Eustace set his teeth and drove the thorn into the Lion's pad. And there came out a great drop of blood, redder than all redness that you have ever seen or imagined. And it splashed into the stream over the dead body of the King. At the same moment the doleful music stopped. And the dead King began to be changed. His white beard turned to gray, and from gray to yellow, and got shorter and vanished altogether; and his sunken cheeks grew round and fresh, and the wrinkles were smoothed, and his eyes opened, and his eyes and lips both laughed, and suddenly he leaped up and stood before them—a very young man, or a boy.[4]

ENDNOTES

1. Augustine, *Confessions*, trans. Thomas Williams (Indianapolis: Hackett, 2019), 53.

2. For references in the Old Testament and for discussion, see Jon D. Levenson, *Resurrection and the Restoration of Israel: The Ultimate Victory of the God of Life* (New Haven, CT: Yale University Press, 2006), 186–87. Levenson takes this relationship between sleep and death more negatively than I do. He understands sleep's similarity to death to mean that sleep itself was considered dangerous, and waking to be a type of miraculous resurrection in which God restores one's soul. Perhaps he is correct that early on the relationship was conceived in this way, that both sleep and death are dangerous, but I suggest that as believers continued to reflect on the relationship, they came to see that the opposite understanding could also be true, *viz.*, that neither sleep nor death were dangerous or permanent.

3. Babylonian Talmud, tractate *Baba Bathra* 57b, quoted in Levenson, *Resurrection*, 74, 186.

4. C. S. Lewis, *The Silver Chair*, The Chronicles of Narnia (New York: HarperCollins, 1953), ch. 16, 252.

BIBLIOGRAPHY

Augustine. *Confessions.* Translated by Thomas Williams. Indianapolis: Hackett, 2019.

Babylonian Talmud, tractate *Baba Bathra* 57b.

Levenson, Jon D. *Resurrection and the Restoration of Israel: The Ultimate Victory of the God of Life.* New Haven, CT: Yale University Press, 2006.

Lewis, C. S. *The Silver Chair.* The Chronicles of Narnia. New York: HarperCollins, 1953.

CHAPTER 10
JESUS'S RESURRECTION

JAMIE COX

Imagine looking at a large canvas that is totally black —the darkest of blacks. Nothing is on the canvas. As you stand before this intensely dark canvas, even the surrounding area becomes black, so black that you literally cannot see your hand in front of your face. You feel alone, isolated, and separated from all you know inside this blackness.

As you continue to stand, you realize everything is turning to scarlet. The canvas that had been so black now has scarlet running from the top, changing the entire surface to scarlet. As you continue to stand there, mesmerized by the changing colors, the canvas—and surrounding area—is now the most brilliant white. Gone is the black. Gone is the scarlet. The canvas and area are whiter than pure snow.

As we gather on the first day of the week to partake of the Lord's Supper, where does your mind take you? Do you envision yourself standing below the cross on which Jesus hung (Luke 23:33)? Do you gaze upward, seeing His body struggling to grasp for air, His face filled with agony and blood still seeping from the open wounds where the thorns of the crown had pierced His head (Matt 27:29)? Do you see the nails that were driven into His hands and feet? Do you see the jagged gaping hole in His side where He was pierced with the spear (John 19:34)? Do you envision the rending of the curtain in the temple or the blackness that came over the earth or the open graves and the once dead walking on the earth again (Matt 27:51–54)? Do you remember the new tomb, the spices that were packed around His body and the linen cloth that kept them close to our Savior's body (John 19:40)? Or do you see tomb, void of the body of Jesus (Mark 16:5–6)? Or Mary Magdalene talking to the one she initially believed to be the gardener (John 20:11–18)? As you partake of the bread that represents His body and the fruit of the vine that represents His blood, what comes to mind? What do you take away from the memorial service each first day of the week?

Jesus was neither the first or last person to be cruelly mistreated and unjustly brought before the courts. Joseph had been imprisoned for no fault of his own (Gen 39:20). Naboth was stoned without a trial based on false accusations (1 Kgs 21). Peter and the other apostles were beaten for preaching the gospel (Acts 5:40). Paul was repeatedly beaten and imprisoned (2 Cor 11:24–28).

Jesus was not the first or last person to be crucified—two others were executed at the same time as Jesus (John 19:18). Crucifixion was a common way to deal with the criminals of the day.

Our Lord was not the first person to be put in a tomb

for burial: the tomb in which He was placed had been prepared for Joseph of Arimathea (Matt 27:57–61). Jesus was not the first to be packed in spices and wrapped in linen (John 19:40).

What made Jesus's death special—and what makes His memorial service memorable?

Some might suggest His resurrection, but that excellent suggestion merits unpacking. The Bible makes clear that resurrection was not something new. Elijah raised the son of the widow of Zarephath from the dead (1 Kgs 17:17–24). Elisha raised the son of the Shunammite woman (2 Kgs 4:18–37). Isaiah had prophesized, "Your dead shall live, their bodies shall rise" (Isa 26:19). Jesus had raised at least four people from death. He raised the child of the widow of Nain (Luke 7:11–17). Jesus had raised Jairus's daughter (Luke 8:49–56). Jesus had raised Lazarus after Lazarus was dead for four days (John 11:39). As Jesus died, God the Father opened many tombs: "And many bodies of the saints who had fallen asleep were raised" (Matt 27:50–53).

What made Jesus's death distinctive—and therefore, should make the Lord's Supper impactful each week? In 1977, Don Francisco answered that question through the words of a very powerful song—"He's Alive." Please bless yourself by taking a few moments to listen to the song.[1] Hearing it provides a rich context for fuller appreciation of this essay.

Jesus rose from the grave never to die again. Jesus's resurrection was unique in that He did not die again and will not die again (Rev 1:18).

In addition to the once-for-all permanence of His resurrection, we must remember its once-for-all unique context. Jesus left heaven and took on flesh knowing that His mission was to die for our sins (Phil 2:5–11). He knew from the start that He was the good shepherd who would give His life for the sheep (John 10:11). He knew from the days of Isaiah that He would be "despised and rejected by men, a man of sorrows and acquainted with grief" (Isa 53:3). He knew that He would bear our griefs, carry our sorrows, and be pierced for our transgressions (Isa 53:4–5). He knew that He would bear our sins in His body on the cross (Isa 53:10–12). Knowing all that and having full power to control His own life, He willingly died for us (John 13:1–5). And He did all this knowing that most people would reject His stunning sacrifice (Matt 7:13–14, Heb 6:4–6). What amazing grace and love!

But there's more to this uniqueness. Jesus was the only sinless human ever to exist (Rom 3:23, 1 Pet 2:21–25). Other innocent men were crucified, but Jesus has the distinction of being the only perfect man to suffer such a fate. Jesus was also the only person to sacrificially surrender His life when He had the power to refuse (John 10:17–18) and to do so for those who were His enemies (Rom 5:6–8). On top of that, He made this sacrifice joyfully (Heb 12:1–2).

Some of the Corinthians struggled with the concept of the resurrection. They questioned both its reality and its importance. Paul confidently assured them that the resurrection of Jesus was real and fundamental in importance.

> For I delivered to you as of first importance what I also received: that Christ died for our sins in accordance with the Scriptures, that He was buried, that He was raised on

the third day in accordance with the Scriptures and that
He appeared to Cephas, then to the twelve (1 Cor 15:3–5).

In that one sentence is the gospel—the good news
—proclaimed.

Paul presents the truth of 1 Corinthians 15:3–5 as not
just important, but of first importance—paramount, critical, crucial. Jesus died for our sins (Col 2:13–14). Jesus was
buried. Jesus rose on the third day. Jesus's resurrection is
the cornerstone on which Christians can place our confidence. Without the resurrection, there is no faith (1 Cor
15:14). Without Jesus's resurrection, man still lives in sin (1
Cor 15:17). Man is still separated from God. Man is still
living in blackness, alone, without faith, and without hope.
Death becomes the end. Death has a major sting. Without
the resurrection of Jesus, Christians are most miserable
and most to be pitied (1 Cor 15:19). Our existence makes no
sense. We have no future.

Jesus's resurrection allows us to have faith. "Now faith
is the assurance of things hoped for, the conviction of
things not seen" (Heb 11:1). With the faith that His resurrection provides us, we can be obedient to God: "And
without faith it is impossible to please Him ..." (Heb 11:6).
By striving to be obedient to God, we have hope: hope that
God will grant us strength (Eph 3:14–21 & 6:10), hope that
we can endure all things (Phil 4:13), hope that God will
bless us (2 Pet 1:2–3), hope that God will provide for us, and
hope of eternal life in His presence (Heb 6:12–20).

Jesus's resurrection takes the sting out of death. Death
is no longer the end or something to be feared or dreaded.
Death is not the conclusion of life. Death leads to the

imperishable and immortal. Death becomes something that is embraced, longed for, sought after. There is no victory in death itself in that death is not the conclusion. As Paul quotes Isaiah,

> 'Death is swallowed up in victory. O death, where is your victory? O death, where is your sting?' The sting of death is sin, and the power of sin is the law. But thanks be to God, who gives us the victory through our Lord Jesus Christ (1 Cor 15:55–57).

Death becomes simply a passage to a brighter, fuller, and more exciting existence.

Jesus's resurrection takes the finality of death out of the equation. Jesus's resurrection opens the door to the joys of life eternal, an everlasting life in the presence of God, the Creator of all, and His Son who has received all things (Matt 28:18). Jesus's resurrection gives us opportunity to focus on a place where there is no sin, no sorrow, no pain, no sadness, and no tears (Rev 21:4). Jesus's resurrection gives us the occasion to envision heaven and all its splendor, knowing that its glories and beauty are so far greater than we can imagine (Rev 21:15–27).

Jesus's resurrection gives us greater knowledge of God's love for us. While "for God so loved the world, that he gave his only Son, that whoever believes in him should not perish but have eternal life" (John 3:16) is one of the more recognizable passages in Scripture, God's giving of His Son is just the beginning. Through Jesus's resurrection, God offers glorious wonders and countless blessings. His resurrection opens the door for the opportunity to live in the presence of God, to approach His throne face to face, to know and feel the immeasurableness of His love for us (Rom 5:1–11).

The new life we have through the resurrection not only makes death simply a passageway, Jesus's resurrection gives us a new life—a life that has us living for Him. Through this new life, He not only displays to us His love for us but allows us to glorify Him by showing others His love for all (2 Cor 4:16–5:21). We are able to long for the body that is spiritual, pure and like Jesus Himself. We put off the old man of sin and separation from God.

Our lives are the blackness on the canvas, filled with the darkness that comes with shame, sin, and hopelessness. The blackness is the separation from God who exists only in the light (Eph 5:8–14). Scarlet is the blood of Jesus as He hung on the cross—that blood flows over our lives, washing our sins away.

Remember that you were at that time separated from Christ, alienated from the commonwealth of Israel and strangers to the covenants of promise, having no hope and without God in the world. But now in Christ Jesus you who once were far off have been brought near by the blood of Jesus (Eph 2:12–13).

White is the purity that Jesus's resurrection gives us.

Come now, let us reason together, says the Lord: though your sins are like scarlet, they shall be as white as snow; though they are red like crimson, they shall become like wool (Isa 1:18).

As we gather on the first day of each week to break the

bread and drink the cup, yes, our minds should return to the cross and see our Brother, Friend, Savior, and Redeemer hanging there with the horrors that He endured, but only for a brief moment. Our minds should swiftly turn to the glorious, wondrous, hope-filled knowledge that Jesus is neither still on the cross nor in the tomb. He arose, He ascended, and He rules by the right hand of the Father. He intercedes and mediates for us until the time of His return (Rom 8:33, 1 Tim 2:5–6). He lives as our permanent propitiation, our perfect atoning sacrifice (Heb 7:25, 1 John 2:1–2).

We would never suggest downplaying the miraculous birth of our Lord (Luke 2), but Jesus did not remain a baby: "Jesus increased in wisdom and stature and in favor with God and man (Luke 2:52). To think only of baby Jesus is to neglect His service, teaching, example, and sacrificial death. Similarly, to focus only on the cross is to miss God's most glorious and important act. God the Father raised our Savior. And our Savior has changed the blackness of sin in our lives to the whiteness of perfect purity because HE IS ALIVE.

ENDNOTES

1. https://www.youtube.com/watch?v=1DQfthEHVc4.

CHAPTER 11
THE CALL TO DISCIPLESHIP
THE DEMAND

KEITH D. STANGLIN

For what credit is it if, sinning and receiving a beating, you steadfastly endure? But if, doing good and suffering, you steadfastly endure, this grace before God. For to this you were called, because Christ also suffered on your behalf, leaving for you an example so that you might follow in his steps, who did not do sin, nor was deceit found in his mouth, who being reviled did not revile in return, suffering he did not make threats, but handed himself over to him who judges righteously; who himself brought up our sins in his body on the tree, so that having died to sins we might live for righteousness, by whose wound you were healed. For you were like sheep gone astray, but you have returned now to the shepherd and overseer of your souls. (1 Pet 2:20–25)

The second-century, apocryphal book, *Acts of Peter*, tells stories about Peter's later ministry in Rome—especially his contests with Simon Magus—filling in the omissions of the first-century records. Toward the end of the book, the story is told of some women believers who learned that the prefect wanted to kill Peter. So Peter's brothers and sisters in Christ warned him to flee the city of Rome, for his safety. Reluctant at first, he followed their advice. On his way out of the city, he met the Lord heading in the opposite direction, toward Rome. Peter asked, "Lord, where are you going?" The Lord replied, "I am going into Rome, to be crucified." "Crucified again?" Peter asked. "Again," the Lord answered. At that moment, Peter "came to himself" and returned to Rome, rejoicing, where he was immediately arrested and then crucified (as the text says, head downward, by his request).[1] Peter heard the call and responded.

Stories like this one from the early church generally stand out to modern readers. Certain aspects of these stories seem alien to contemporary Christian experience. Above all, they reflect a situation of persecution that is foreign to Western Christians and tremendous courage and joy in the face of that persecution. Peter's actions, at least by the end of the tale, present a striking contrast to the way we often approach discipleship, putting a premium on individual freedom and rights and, above all, safety and security.

Here is a case in point. Many years ago, I served as a counselor at an annual day-long retreat for ministry students. Each counselor was assigned to a group of eight to ten students for break-out discussions. I remember asking my group what their plans for ministry were after graduation. The students took their turns and spoke about their dreams for serving in the kingdom.

In my group there was an engaged couple. They said that they planned to move to a small town after they graduated and got married. They said the town's name; it was somewhere in the middle of the United States, though I had never heard of it. In contrast to other students' more open-ended plans for ministry, I was struck by their very specific plan for settling in this town. I inquired further. "Is that where you're from?" No. "Do you have family there?" They did not. "Do you have a job waiting for you?" Negative. Then why did they want to move to that specific town? What seemed like a random decision was actually quite deliberate. They said they had done the research, and this town is statistically the safest place to live in the whole country. It had the lowest rate of crime, the lowest rate of accidents, the lowest rate of violence, and the lowest rate of unnatural death.

I had never heard such a thing. They do seem like reasonable grounds, and people have had worse reasons for moving to a place. But I began thinking aloud about the idea of calling and particularly their calling to ministry. I began to consider with the group the lengths to which people go to be safe and avoid physical death, only to physically die anyway. I grant that the young couple probably did not want to hear these things, which may be why they joined someone else's group after lunch.

The concept of "call" (Latin, *vocatio*), neglected in some ecclesiastical circles, is prominent in the New Testament. It is mentioned in the text at the head of this essay: "to this you were called" (1 Pet 2:21). We know that God calls us for the ultimate purpose of our eternal salvation and fellowship in his glory. But in this life, what is the purpose of the call? To exactly what kind of life are believers called? How would the best-selling, popular Christian books answer this question? Does answering God's call mean a life of happiness, as one writer puts it, our "best life now"? Perhaps the call means the freedom to be "untamed" or that we "expand our borders." Or maybe the call means that we should "empty out the negative."[2] Given the popularity of such books in Christian circles, the question is worth considering.

In general, we can affirm that God calls us so that we will be his covenant people in this life and in the life to come. The covenant people are described in Revelation 14:4 as those who "follow the Lamb wherever he goes." Being his covenant people means following him *wherever* he goes, being a true disciple.

Again, the text from 1 Peter says, "To this you were called, because Christ suffered for you, leaving you an example, that you should follow in his steps" (1 Pet 2:21). Christ is the example, and his people are to "follow in his steps." To follow the Lamb wherever he goes is one way of describing the *demand* of God's call. What should the disciple of Christ expect? What is this discipleship to which he calls us? What does it mean to follow the steps of Jesus?

In a general sense, following in his steps means to do what Jesus would do. Indeed, the modern classic, *In His Steps* (whose title is based on this verse from 1 Peter), tells that much, and rightly so.[3] To follow in his steps certainly entails being pure and holy. Without doubt, it requires service, kindness, and compassion toward others. But what is Peter talking about when he says that Christ is our example? "To this you were called?" To what?

Look back to find the antecedent. "To this," means "to suffering for doing the good" (1 Pet 2:20). Thus, "to [suffering] you were called, because Christ suffered" (1 Pet 2:21). Notice the larger context of these verses. If there is only one thing one should know about the letter called 1 Peter, it is that the letter is about the suffering of the early church. When Peter calls us to follow in Jesus's steps, he is calling us to suffer. When any of God's people suffers as a "Christian," Peter goes on to write, they participate, or share, in Christ's sufferings (1 Pet 4:13–16).

According to Peter, discipleship consists in suffering for doing good. Of course, there's more to being a disciple than mere suffering; nevertheless, suffering is an essential aspect of the demand of the call. If we would answer the call to salvation, it means being prepared for suffering. "But wait!" a modern disciple may protest. "This was not mentioned among the benefits when I became a Christian. Yes, I was told about the joy and self-esteem and the expansion of my borders—that is, that things would be good. But suffering—here and now?" Where did Peter get such a wild notion that discipleship entails suffering?

If such a protest is the gut reaction, then it is no different from that of Peter himself, back when he *first* heard this "wild notion" from Jesus. Three times in the Gospel according to Mark—once each in chapters 8, 9, and 10—the disciples misunderstand what it means to be a disciple, and Jesus then tries to correct their misunderstanding. Each time, the misunderstanding is occasioned by Jesus' prediction of his death.

Note the first instance in Mark 8:27–32. After Jesus predicted his death for the first time, Peter rebuked Jesus. According to Matthew's account, Peter said, "God forbid it, Lord! This will never be for you!" (Matt 16:22). Mark's account, however, omits the words of Peter's rebuke of Jesus. Mark leaves the exact wording to the reader's imagination. Perhaps Peter's words sounded something like this:

"All right, Jesus, now that we're all agreed that you are the Christ, the Messiah, let's get on with the kingdom building. I will *gladly* be your disciple and follow in your steps ... yes ... all the way to the throne and royal palace. We are really going to enjoy ourselves .... What did you say? You're going to Jerusalem to suffer and die? No, that is incompatible with being the Messiah, the king. God's Messiah is meant for glory and honor, not shame and death. You know what the rabbis say, Jesus! Your best life now!"

Whatever his exact words, Peter was definitely reacting negatively to the idea that the Messiah would suffer and die in Jerusalem. Such an outcome, Peter thought, was not to be, and Jesus of all people should have known better. Then, after Peter's rebuke, Jesus responded: "Get behind me, Satan, because you are not thinking the things of God but the things of men" (Mark 8:33). Jesus then added, "If anyone wants to follow behind me, let him deny himself and take up his cross and follow me" (Mark 8:34).

What does Jesus mean when he says to take up your cross and follow me? The command is less complex than we sometimes make it. The cross is not a symbol for a little hardship of life, imposed as part of ordinary existence, that one would seek to avoid. The cross is not the traffic jam on the way to work. Rather, pick up your cross, *voluntarily*. Even if one has now heard it a thousand times, it would sound very strange the first time. A modern analogy might be: "Pick up your extension cord, and follow me to the electric chair." Is there any doubt about the meaning of this instruction and where it ends? Even this analogy does not quite convey the shame and offense of the first-century *stauros*, *crux*, cross (see, for example, 1 Cor 1:18–2:5).[4]

When Jesus calls his disciples to take up their cross and follow him, where did he just say he was going? To suffer and die. It is explicit in the next verse—saving one's life requires giving it up (Mark 8:35). Jesus had already flipped Peter's worldview on its head—not earthly glory, not "emptying out the negative," but suffering and death are the path for God's Messiah. Yet the real disconcerting point to Peter is this: not only suffering and death for the *Messiah*, the king, but for you, too, his subjects—that is, if you truly want to be his disciple. This realization is what shakes Peter and the disciples to the core. And it ought to do the same to all Christians. As Dietrich Bonhoeffer put it, "When Christ calls a man, he bids him come and die."[5]

Make no mistake about it. Physical safety is not named as one of the priorities of discipleship. Moderns promote "safety first." The disciples who heard Jesus's words for the first time were not so different. They evidently were not enthused to learn that the path they were choosing was the opposite of safety and security; it was the way of danger, risk, and trust. The question in the Gospel of Mark is: Would they trust? The eventual answer is: No (Mark 14:50).

The more mature Peter, writing in 1 Peter 2, eventually

came to realize that we are indeed called for the ultimate goal of salvation and glory, but only by means of suffering and cross. The glory comes on the other side of suffering.

If *we* want to be disciples of Christ, then we must answer the same call to discipleship. The more mature among us—like the older, wiser Peter—realize the demands that this call entails. At the same time, the less mature among us—like the younger Peter and sometimes myself— tend to seek out happiness, "living a life you love," expanding our borders.

Believers in the global West may never face the decision of dying for Christ, a possibility that many millions face in the world every day. But, as his disciples, we must be dying for Christ every day, "taking up the cross *daily*," as Luke records it (Luke 9:23). And with Luke's addition of that word, the call to crucifixion evolves more clearly into a metaphor for quotidian life, not only the one-time choice but also the daily decision. Yet its message must never lose its meaning and power. Christians are called to put to death all selfishness, to spend their lives in service to God, and to be prepared to suffer. When we live for God, when we are willing to carry a cross, this means not always, by default, seeking the safest place to live, but instead seeking the place where God can use us most in his service.

A life devoted to service and discipleship does not mean comfort, at least not as most of the best-selling Christian books usually define it. It means talking to people one may not be comfortable talking to or going places one is not used to visiting or living in. It means spending our free time in selfless giving. Disciples of Jesus will help the homeless, visit the prisons, do an act of kindness for someone they don't know or owe, find the loneliest person they can and make a new friend, or give up a night of TV to spend time with God.

To bear one's own cross may not be for one's salvation —only Jesus's cross accomplishes that. But taking up the cross is for our sanctification, an indication of whom we are following and of who truly reigns in our lives.

It could be that a person is still thinking that this life of discipleship sounds burdensome. Didn't Jesus say that he would make the yoke easy and the burden light? (Matt 11:30). That is true. But the promise is that, with the help of God's Spirit, the *heavy cross* becomes light. Bonhoeffer writes, "The command of Jesus is hard, unutterably hard, for those who try to resist it. But for those who willingly submit, the yoke is easy, and the burden is light."[6] What starts out being uncomfortable becomes a privilege, truly your best life.

Peter agrees. He writes that this calling to do what is good, to suffer for it, and to steadfastly endure in it, is "grace before God" (1 Pet 2:20). In other words, in God's judgment, this way of life is truly a gift, to live for something that is worth dying for. As such, the persecuted are in fact blessed to have the kingdom of heaven (Matt 5:10). In this way, Peter, who at first scorned the idea of the cross and was roundly rebuked for it, in the end, followed the Lamb wherever he goes, and finally embraced his own cross with joy.

May God give us all the grace to respond to his call to be not mere admirers, but followers, imitators, disciples, true servants—the call to self-sacrificially follow the Lamb wherever he goes, the call that leads through suffering to glorious salvation in Christ. May God bless all his people toward this end.

ENDNOTES

1. See *Acts of Peter*, 35–40, in M. R. James, *The Apocryphal New Testament* (Oxford: Clarendon Press, 1924), 333–36. The Latin translation of Peter's initial question, "Quo vadis?" has become a justly famous representation of this verbal exchange and its consequences. It was a later tradition that gave the reason for Peter's unusual request to be crucified inversely—namely, his unworthiness to be crucified in the same manner as Jesus.

2. I do not recommend the books from which this language is directly derived, except to see the kinds of books that frequently sit atop the "Christian Best-sellers" lists. Someone must be reading them. See Joel Osteen, *Your Best Life Now: 7 Steps to Living at Your Full Potential* (New York: FaithWords, 2004); Glennon Doyle, *Untamed* (New York: The Dial Press, 2020); Bruce Wilkinson, *The Prayer of Jabez: Breaking through to the Blessed Life* (Colorado Springs: Multnomah Books, 2000); Joel Osteen, *Empty Out the Negative: Make Room for More Joy, Greater Confidence, and New Levels of Influence* (New York: FaithWords, 2020).

3. Charles M. Sheldon, *In His Steps* (1896; repr., Grand Rapids: Revell, 1984). This was the Christian best-seller of a more discerning generation not so long ago, but a world apart.

4. For a classic statement of the scandal of the cross, see Martin Hengel, *Crucifixion in the Ancient World and the*

Folly of the Message of the Cross (Philadelphia: Fortress Press, 1977).

5. Dietrich Bonhoeffer, *The Cost of Discipleship*, rev. ed. (New York: MacMillan, 1959), 99.

6. Bonhoeffer, *Discipleship*, 40.

BIBLIOGRAPHY

Acts of Peter, 35–40. Pages 333–36 in *The Apocryphal New Testament*. Translated by M. R. James. Oxford: Clarendon Press, 1924.

BONHOEFFER, DIETRICH. *THE COST OF DISCIPLESHIP*. Rev. ed. New York: MacMillan, 1959.

DOYLE, GLENNON. *UNTAMED*. NEW YORK: THE DIAL Press, 2020.

HENGEL, MARTIN. *CRUCIFIXION IN THE ANCIENT WORLD and the Folly of the Message of the Cross*. Philadelphia: Fortress Press, 1977.

OSTEEN, JOEL. *EMPTY OUT THE NEGATIVE: MAKE ROOM for More Joy, Greater Confidence, and New Levels of Influence*. New York: FaithWords, 2020.

_____. *YOUR BEST LIFE NOW: 7 STEPS TO LIVING AT YOUR Full Potential*. New York: FaithWords, 2004.

SHELDON, CHARLES M. *IN HIS STEPS*. 1896 REPR. GRAND Rapids: Revell, 1984.

WILKINSON, BRUCE. *THE PRAYER OF JABEZ: BREAKING through to the Blessed Life*. Colorado Springs: Multnomah Books, 2000.

SCRIPTURE INDEX

CREDITS

HERITAGE LEGACY SERIES

The Heritage Legacy Series follows the longstanding academic tradition of the festschrift, a collection of essays in recognition of a respected colleague. Biblically, it embodies the principles of giving honor to whom honor is due and esteeming godly servants for their work. HCU Press is happy to show appreciation to those who have blessed Heritage Christian University and the church in countless ways.

Things Most Surely Believed: Festschrift in Honor of Charlie Wayne Kilpatrick edited by Heritage Christian University Press.

Serving the Lord: Festschrift in Honor of Freddie Patrick Moon and Janet Stewart Moon edited by Heritage Christian University Press.

CYPRESS
PUBLICATIONS
An Imprint of Heritage Christian University Press

To see full catalog of Heritage Christian University Press and its imprint Cypress Publications, visit www. hcu.edu/publications